Praise for *How to Talk to Anyone at Work*

This powerful, practical book shows you how to influence others, communicate clearly, and achieve your goals through others faster than ever before.

—BRIAN TRACY, America's #1 expert on
business relationships and bestselling author

This outstanding—and fun to read—book teaches you ways to reach the top without making enemies along the way!

—MARSHALL GOLDSMITH, Thinkers50
"World's Most Influential Leadership Thinker"
and author of the *New York Times* bestseller *Triggers*

To avoid your career failing to launch, Leil Lowndes's new book should be required reading for every employee. Reasoned, researched, and real—it's a fun, relatable, quick read with practical tips and advice that everyone can and should use immediately!

—GREGORY GIANGRANDE, career advice columnist
for the *New York Post*

This is the kind of book you don't just read, but always keep around to refer to. It's a playbook to handle the multitude of communication challenges we all face. I highly recommend it to anyone who wants to be a masterful communicator.

—RICK BRINKMAN, coauthor of *Dealing with People You Can't Stand*

Like a sure-footed guide who shows up in the nick of time, Leil Lowndes charts a path for professional success in our dizzying digital age. *How to Talk to Anyone at Work* is jammed with more usable insights than books twice its size—you'll find an idea to implement on every page. Get this book, use the ideas, and reap the benefits of better communication.

—GEOFFREY TUMLIN, author of *Stop Talking, Start Communicating*

Lowndes opens our eyes by having us look at our core human connections with an unprecedented depth. Her advice is subtle and powerful. A great and necessary read for those who want to get ahead at work.

—KATHI ELSTER, coauthor of *Working with You Is Killing Me*

Leil's new book is filled with gems of communication techniques to help you reach the top and stay there, without making any enemies along the way—an enviable skill!

—DEBRA FINE, author of *The Fine Art of Small Talk*

Leil Lowndes has done it again! Her previous book *How to Talk to Anyone* showed you how your life can improve if you master basic communication skills. This one goes deeper and shows you how those same skills—and new ones—can help you prosper professionally. They are simple, but not trivial. Leil has done a super job of making their value come alive through powerful anecdotes. This book is a keeper. Reread a few pages from time to time and implement what she recommends.

—SRIKUMAR RAO, author of *Happiness at Work*

Whether you're dealing with your boss, a coworker, your team, or the entire company, Leil gives you 72 remarkable ways to get what you want and earn everyone's esteem through superior communicating.

—CRAIG WEBER, author of *Conversational Capacity*

Leil, who has addressed audiences from 10 to 10,000, knows how vital making presentations is in today's workplace. She gives you superb advice on how to squelch the butterflies and present with passion.

—JEREMEY DONOVAN, author of *How to Deliver a TED Talk*

If you want to hit home runs with your boss, coworkers, and clients, read *How to Talk to Anyone at Work*. It's a winner and you will be, too, when you follow her savvy career advice.

—DON GABOR, author of *How to Start a Conversation and Make Friends*

Read this and learn from the best! Leil's new book is a gem and teaches you how to achieve what many believe is an impossible task—being both liked and respected by everyone at work.

—OLIVIA FOX CABANE, author of *The Charisma Myth*

Leil Lowndes paints a picture of what too many of us face at work: toxic bosses, backstabbing coworkers, office politics run amuck. If only we could make all of those realities go away. Well, they're not going away anytime soon, so our only choice is to figure out a better way to respond. *How to Talk to Anyone at Work* delivers on just that. With a delightful and easy-to-read style, Lowndes arms us with useful tricks to communicate in a way that finally gets us the respect we deserve. If you want to get ahead, be more productive, and be a whole lot happier on the job, this book is for you. I highly recommend it!

—LAURA PUTNAM, author of *Workplace Wellness That Works*

If you read only one self-help book this year, pick up this extraordinary and enjoyable must-read primer. It's written for you to get to the top and stay there.

—DEBRA BENTON, author of *How to Act Like a CEO*

Leil Lowndes has done a magnificent job describing all the interpersonal challenges in the workplace and what do about them. Having led a job stress group for 15 years, I would highly recommend this book to my clients!

—JOHN ARDEN, PhD, ABPP, author of *Surviving Job Stress*

A great book that recognizes the role nonverbal communication plays in your success. Leil gives you specific and concrete information to improve your communication.

—PATTI WOOD, author of *SNAP*

A must-read with excellent advice and tips. Most of us don't think enough about the people portion of our jobs—but it is the most critical to our success. In *How to Talk to Anyone at Work*, Leil Lowndes provides practical advice on how to break down communication barriers at work to make our jobs more enjoyable and rewarding.

—Dr. Noelle Nelson, author of *Got a Bad Boss?*

How to Talk to Anyone at Work provides you with a platinum key to unlock the door to personal and corporate success. Leil's one-of-a-kind tips are terrific.

—Dr. Tony Alessandra, author of *The Platinum Rule*

Leil Lowndes's *How to Talk to Anyone at Work* is a delightful, fun read with lots of practical tips for communicating effectively in the workplace. Leil's warm, personal style combined with her insightful suggestions provides a sense of energy and empowerment that leads you to conclude, "I can do this!"

—Paul White, PhD, coauthor of *The Vibrant Workplace*

Your working life is about to change for the better, and chances are that of your colleagues will, too. Leil gives you engaging one-on-one practical and jargon-free coaching you can apply in an instant. With this advice, how much better an experience might the workplace be?

—Neil Usher, author of *The Elemental Workplace: How to Create a Fantastic Workplace for Everyone*

How to Talk to Anyone at Work gives the reader a manual on how to be successful at work and in life. The guiding principles used in the book are based on confidence with others, showing others you care, clarity in communication, truthfulness to establish credibility, and coexisting patiently with people in an early learning curve. The book matches our own research and recommended practices, especially when the author writes brilliantly about the nonverbal and visual aspects of communication that can be perceived by others as secure, honest, and self-engaged—or not.

—PETER J. DEAN AND MOLLY D. SHEPARD,
authors of *The Bully-Proof Workplace*

HOW TO
TALK TO
ANYONE

AT WORK

72 *Little Tricks for Big Success*

COMMUNICATING ON THE JOB

LEIL LOWNDES

NEW YORK   CHICAGO   SAN FRANCISCO
ATHENS   LONDON   MADRID
MEXICO CITY   MILAN   NEW DELHI
SINGAPORE   SYDNEY   TORONTO

1 2 3 4 5 6 7 8 9   QFR   23 22 21 20 19 18

ISBN   978-1-260-10843-9
MHID   1-260-10843-0

e-ISBN   978-1-260-10844-6
e-MHID   1-260-10844-9

Library of Congress Cataloging-in-Publication Data

Names: Lowndes, Leil, author.
Title: How to talk to anyone at work: 72 little tricks for big success in
    business relationships / Leil Lowndes.
Description: 1 Edition. | New York : McGraw-Hill Education, 2018.
Identifiers: LCCN 2018029784 | ISBN 9781260108439 (paperback) |
    ISBN 1260108430
Subjects: LCSH: Business communication. | BISAC: BUSINESS &
    ECONOMICS / Business Communication / General.
Classification: LCC HF5718 .L69 2018 | DDC 650.1/3—dc23
LC record available at https://lccn.loc.gov/2018029784

McGraw-Hill Education books are available at special quantity dis-
counts to use as premiums and sales promotions or for use in corporate
training programs. To contact a representative, please visit the Contact
Us pages at www.mhprofessional.com.

To my many thousands of amazing seminar students, clients, and readers, who shared challenges they faced with their bosses, colleagues, reports, and customers—I learned as much from you as you did from me, and together, we found solutions.

Contents

Contents

Contents

Contents

Contents

Acknowledgments

Have you ever thought about writing a book? We all have, and those of us crazy enough to go through with it know it's like suddenly having not only a new partner, but being pregnant and having hundreds of people from your past move into your home at the same time. Your new "partner" criticizes you all day long and complains you're never working hard enough. The "baby" you're carrying awakens you several times a night kicking, and the only way to get back to sleep is to scribble a few notes in the dark—which are indecipherable in the morning. And the hordes of people now living with you are the characters in your book (in my case, very real people from the past).

But it's more than worth it! When you finally turn in the manuscript, ecstasy floods through you as you realize how much you've drained out of yourself to share with your readers. The immense reward is knowing the many ways it will benefit them.

Writing a book is never a solo accomplishment, of course. Along with my clients and wonderful seminar students, I'm grateful to several people in my personal life who held my hand during the labor pains.

My beloved partner, Giorgio Accornero, who cheerfully did the shopping, cooking, and even cleaning, so I could pursue this journey.

Chris Coomes, a visionary and top manager at Google, who gave me a peek into tomorrow's amazing workplace which I'll share with you at the end of the book. *Spoiler:* You'll have your own virtual assistant doing most of the grunge tasks, work with augmented reality, enjoy a more collaborative, less structured environment, maybe even work from home or wherever you like. It's a nice life—if you code it right! (Coding will be a required second language.)

My friend Gary M. Krebs, who urged me to write this book and openly shared his vast knowledge of corporate challenges—from being a new employee through becoming the top boss. Gary now runs a successful company, GMK Writing and Editing, and brings his 30 years of publishing experience to his clients.

I'll always be thankful to my dear friend Phil Perry, whom some of you met in my previous books, for his constant willingness to serve as an editorial sounding board.

Lisa Queen, my marvelous agent who was with me from conception through delivery. And of course my editor at McGraw-Hill, Casey Ebro, who, with a single phone call, turned my life around for a full year by inviting me to write this. She gently and skillfully guided the book into the form she knew would be invaluable for readers seeking success and satisfaction on the job.

Introduction

HOW TO TALK TO ANYONE AT WORK:
LITTLE TRICKS FOR BIG SUCCESS
COMMUNICATING ON THE JOB

Some people have it all. Everyone at work admires them. They easily turn colleagues into friends, bosses into backers, and prospects into buyers. They get special treatment, raises, and promotions. People respect them, and they get to the top fast. What's their secret? You'll soon find out.

Perhaps so far you haven't been that fortunate at work. Most people aren't. You may be stuck with a boss who constantly criticizes you, is a control freak, micromanager, or just plain jerk. I'm sure there are a couple of coworkers who drive you berserk due to their gossiping, bullying, or backstabbing. If you're the boss, you may have a few reports who make you want to tear your hair out—or theirs! And who hasn't had customers they'd like to strangle because they're nitpickers, know-it-alls, or are never satisfied.

When you were a kid, nothing prepared you for these workplace characters, because, hopefully, you had parents and relatives who believed in you and complimented you when you did something good. You had teachers who encouraged you, listened to you, and didn't secretly hope you'd fail. You had friends you trusted and enjoyed being around. Of course you ran into the usual assortment of bullies and creeps, but you didn't have to deal with them eight hours a day, five days a week. And you didn't need to watch every word coming out of your mouth for fear of consequences. So when you graduated, you assumed your job wouldn't be all that different. Maybe you even looked forward to your adventures in the working world and expected it to be a supportive and somewhat pleasant environment.

But then, POW! What happened at work probably astonished you. Nothing prepared you for the challenges you'd confront nor the crazies you'd have to deal with. I'm sure they gave you a job description, but I bet no one gave you the bottom line on the difficult people, cliques, and complicated corporate culture. You wanted to ask someone who'd been there longer to give you the scoop, but you feared too many questions might make you look stupid. No doubt you saw some of your new colleagues acting unprofessionally and others doing things behind the boss's back. Maybe even your boss was goofing off or accused you of something you didn't do. But you didn't dare speak up for fear of being fired.

The dynamic of the workplace is different from that of real life. You're not just dealing with an individual at work; you must factor in his or her position, prejudices, boss, and relationship with everyone else in the company. You must also do it in a "second language" through e-mail, texts, chat applications, and videoconferencing. Some of you must work with augmented reality or whatever new technology your particular job involves.

OK, I've painted a grim picture of the workplace, and I hope you don't feel like you're looking down a gun barrel at *your* job. But during my several decades of consulting and teaching public and in-house corporate seminars to thousands of employees and supervisors, I've heard a myriad of disaster stories. Truth is stranger than fiction, especially at work. No matter what you do or where you earn your living, your work can be either a dream job or a nightmare. It's all up to you.

"Up to me?" you ask. "Why? My bosses and coworkers are the ones who are the problem." Yes, they probably are. But with one incredible and learnable skill, you can change the way people treat you, increase your happiness, and boost your chances of getting ahead. It won't happen overnight, but I'll share a plan that you can start using the minute you walk into work tomorrow morning. If you follow the 72 techniques, which I like to call "little tricks," it will make bosses respect you, colleagues more congenial, and your reports more dedicated. *The bottom line:* Life on the job will be more pleasant, productive, and successful.

What's the Number One Skill You Need?

You guessed it: whether it's online or in person, it's the rare ability *to communicate effectively with everyone in your place of employment.* I'm not just talking about regular communication skills, the kind people need to get along in everyday life. I'm talking about specific techniques necessary for success on the job. It doesn't matter whether you're employed by—or run—a big corporation, a medium-size company, or a small business, a factory, retail, or family business. The techniques work in every type of organization.

I'm sure you've heard bosses solemnly decree (as though they're the first person to ever say it), "It's a problem with communication." Well, duh, they're right. But everyone thinks the communication problem is with other people, not them. "If only *they* didn't do that." "If only *they* didn't think that way." "If only *they* weren't so stubborn," ". . . so stupid," ". . . so mean," ". . . so irritating," ". . . so (whatever)."

When the communication problem starts to affect the bottom line, that's when management gets involved. The top dogs start barking and sending memos about the importance of "better communication." Or they establish a policy of more meetings. Or fewer meetings. Or no meetings. Oops, they discover none of those worked! Then they say, "What about bringing in a consultant or sending employees to seminars?" Too expensive? "Hmm, what about online seminars and training?" Sure, seminars where employees can sit solo in front of a computer and learn how to deal face-to-face with other human beings? That makes a lot of sense, doesn't it? Sadly, no.

They miss this crucial point: to communicate deeply and effectively with colleagues and bosses, you must make them feel you understand and respect each of them individually. Encouraging the people you work with to open up and paving the path for them to listen to you is crucial. If you accomplish this with everyone, you will be an excellent communicator at work, even while making challenging presentations.

Be assured this is not just another book about dealing with difficult people. Of course you'll meet some of those disagreeable types here. But too much has already been written on how to silence and squash those walking-talking headaches. This book is unique, because you'll learn exceptional skills that get right to the *gut* of the problem. If you start using these tips early in your relationships with everyone at work, you'll prevent problems from developing in the first place. If your issues with certain individuals have already started, I'll show you how to turn those unpleasant relationships around. That way you won't be part of the legions of people who hate their jobs. (That's 70 percent according to a recent *Forbes* survey!) It won't happen overnight, but if you stick with it, the results are guaranteed.

I Hate My Job!

Sadly, over the years I've heard it all: "I hate my job." "I hate my boss." "I hate my coworkers." "I hate my schedule." "I hate my customers," ". . . the commute," ". . . the computer"—". . . the office copier!" I often start my seminars for employees (whose bosses had forced them to attend) by asking, "How many of you are happy to be here today?" A few tentatively raise their hands just to be polite. But then I ask, "How many of you are happy to be out of the office today?" This time, hands all over the room instantly shoot up. We all laugh. Including me. But inside I feel extremely sad.

That's not the way a job should be! Your work should make you feel fulfilled and valued. You deserve to be rewarded in more ways than with money. You deserve to be appreciated for the work you do and the many hours you give the company. Your job should bring you a sense of satisfaction and many joyful moments during the day. So what kept so many of my seminar attendees from feeling that way? The answer was universal. Practically all of them told me it was problems with individuals they had to work with, whether their bosses, direct reports, colleagues, or customers.

What do all these answers have in common? Right, they're all *people*—people you just happen to work with. Many of you read my book *How to Talk to Anyone: 92 Little Tricks for Big Success in Relationships.* There I gave you tips primarily for social situations and making friends, but countless readers tell me how many of the techniques also help them on the job.

Much to my delight, *How to Talk to Anyone* became a bestseller and is still topping the charts in 26 countries around the world. How rewarding it is to know that the basic people skills I shared apply to diverse cultures. Countless readers wrote to tell me how the techniques changed their lives. If you are one of those who contacted me, please know that receiving your messages is one of the greatest joys in my life. Hearing your experiences and those of thousands of my seminar participants inspired me to write this book.

Imagine how thrilled I was when I got a call from my publisher, McGraw-Hill, asking if I'd write a sequel dealing with business situations. You've heard of those near-death phenomena when someone's entire life flashes through his or her mind? Well, right there on the phone, it seemed like my past 20-plus years of consulting and giving seminars on corporate communication skills instantaneously raced through my head. In a heartbeat, I realized I had to write *How to Talk to Anyone at Work*.

First, I reflected on my own experiences and struggles entering the working world and on the thousands of professional challenges my clients and seminar students reported. I reread hundreds of your e-mails detailing your problems on the job. While writing this book, I also consulted with professionals from a wide variety of fields who provided their horror stories and the communication techniques they'd tried. You'll soon meet some of these folks and hear about their successes, disasters, and what they did to eventually get good results. Naturally, I've disguised their names and organizations, but the people, the problems, and the industries they work in are very real.

This book won't help you change the more challenging individuals at work into better people. It doesn't mean horrible bosses will suddenly realize the error of their ways and treat everyone with respect. Natural-born betrayers won't give up their backstabbing ways, and flaunting flatterers won't stop conspicuously playing up to you. Liars won't suddenly discover the virtue of truth, and protesters won't turn into Pollyannas. Know-it-alls won't decide to be humble, braggarts won't convert to modesty, and mean colleagues will stay mean. But even if you can't change the qualities of those characters, here is my promise. When you employ these little tricks, your unsavory coworkers will save their nasty behaviors for others. In fact, they won't even think of using their sinister ways on you because, beginning with the first tip, you'll start earning their esteem and warmth no matter how long you've been working with them. You'll discover ways to turn your work relationships around in a fraction of the time it took for any existing negativity to develop.

Would You Be Happier If You Never Had to Work Again?

Most people, without a second thought, would shout yes! But minor details like making a living, supporting a family, having a roof over your head, and enjoying a few luxuries decree that most of us don't have the choice. A sixth-century BC philosopher had the answer to the dilemma of work. Confucius declared, "Choose a job you love, and you will never have to work a day in your life."

Hmm, I'd have to ponder the abstract and metaphysical aspects of the word "work" before I could say, "Spot on,

Confucius." But I do know that if you can turn the job you have into one you love, you've taken a big step in the right direction. That truly is possible, because in most cases it's the people we work with that make our jobs gratifying or grueling.

Another reason writing this book was thrilling is that so much has happened in the years since I wrote *How to Talk to Anyone*. We now communicate in ways that never existed to the extent they do now. Even today in some sectors, picking up the phone or dropping by someone's desk to talk things out seems primitive. Digital dominates! The modes of communicating—e-mail, texting, social media, chats, video-conferencing, augmented reality to show your ideas, and more—continue to evolve.

A Very Personal Reason I Said Yes to This Book

Don't laugh, but I have always been fascinated by offices! I know that sounds bizarre, but I'm dead serious. This unusual attraction started when I was about six years old. My dad was in advertising, and because both my parents worked, he sometimes took me to his job on snow days, when school was canceled. I'll never forget how cool the copywriters and executives looked in their dark suits, crisp white shirts, and skinny neckties. I was dazzled by the secretaries walking by in slim skirts and taking shorthand for their male bosses.

Does that sound like a late 1960s scene out of the hit TV show *Mad Men*? Yes, that's exactly what it was like. And in my unenlightened immaturity, I loved it. Never mind that it was shamefully sexist and chauvinistic. I wasn't old enough to understand that. Gratefully, the Don Draper era is history, and thanks to *Mad Men*, we can now roll our eyes and shake our heads.

When the kids in my neighborhood went out to play, my girlfriends would squeal, "Let's play house!" Then they'd look around and ask, "Who wants to be the mommy?" And "Who wants to be the daddy?" Because I was something of a tomboy, they'd usually ask me to play the latter. But I didn't want to be the daddy. Or the mommy. Or the baby. I hated playing house. I wanted to "play office."

My favorite toy in the whole world was a red plastic rotary dial telephone with an ear-shattering *brrring* ringtone. It was music to my ears. I loved sitting at my "desk," an old cabinet door placed across the seats of two chairs. When I could talk the other kids into playing office, I'd quickly ask (before they changed their minds), "Who's going to play the boss, and who's going to play the secretary?" I didn't care which role I had. I just loved being in my "office."

But then my childhood fantasy workplace didn't have domineering bosses, exasperating colleagues, or disappointing direct reports. In my imaginary job, there were no office politics, no promotions or demotions, no unspoken rules, no fear of getting fired, no strict chain of command, and no negativity or dysfunctional corporate culture. And there was no miscommunication. It was just a game, and nothing was at stake. But your job is not a game. It's real life, and a lot is at stake.

What About You?

What do you want from your job? Is professional success and shimmying up the totem pole your goal? Do you long for that view from the top? Do you relish being conductor of the symphony, the maestro directing your employees to produce a beautiful product or service?

If so, I hope you realize the top of the peak is not the enviable position it's often cracked up to be. The air is thinner at those heights, and it's harder to breathe. You're treading on a tightrope with few safety nets. One misstep can cause you to crash to the ground. And the larger the company, the longer your descent—meaning the harder you'll hit. One professional bad choice or personal indiscretion has tripped up many a top leader, and a tumble from those heights can mangle you beyond repair.

Suppose reaching the peak is not your goal. All you ask is happiness at work, fulfillment from your career, and the satisfaction of a job well done. Actually, you're the lucky ones. But even to get that, you have to play your cards right. You must learn how to recover from slips, avoid the traps, and get on with the business of being valuable to your company, your family, your friends, and most of all yourself. Happily, the way to achieve this goal is to make smooth moves in five crucial categories which I call the "Five Cs."

Confidence

If you don't have confidence in yourself, how can you expect others to? In this section you'll find ways to gently show everyone that you are 100 percent self-assured from the moment you meet them and throughout your working relationship.

Caring

"People don't care how much you know until they know how much you care" should be gospel in the workplace. Sadly, it seldom is. Here you'll find ways to convince everyone at work that you sincerely care about them and the company.

Clarity

At work, you can't leave clear communication to chance. The stakes are too high! When explaining something to a colleague, have you been tempted to scream, "I know you believe you understand what you think I said, but I'm not sure you realize that what you heard is not what I meant." Very few have found the solution to this persistent dilemma. I'll help you with that, whether you're the speaker or the listener.

Credibility

Speaking without credibility is like talking to the wind. Your words are worthless, and no one will listen if they don't believe you—and in you. In this section you'll find techniques to win the trust and respect of everyone you work with.

Coexistence (with Cruel Bosses and Crazy Colleagues)

Wouldn't work be great if it weren't for the people? Well, for the foreseeable future, flesh-and-blood human beings are here to stay. We'll tackle some of the most troublesome types and talk about how to deal with them, so no one comes out emotionally or professionally destroyed. And today, it's even tougher because you must demonstrate these five crucial success characteristics in a web-based world. Let's get started!

PART I

CONFIDENCE

Your Confidence (or Lack of It) Stands Out Like a Fly in the Sugar Bowl

Why is exuding self-assurance so important? Well, who has known you longer than anyone else? Who has been with you every moment of every day since you were born? Who has observed everything you have ever said and done in life? That's right, *you*. So only you know better than anyone else that your actions merit confidence.

Even if you have deep-rooted insecurities (almost everybody does), you don't want to reveal them at work. You must look like you are sure you can accomplish whatever you want. Unfortunately, when you're fearful or insecure, a myriad of changes take place in your body, and they're hard to hide. As soon as colleagues see you, they can sense anxiety like a dog sniffs fear. However, two-legged upright creatures do the detective work with their eyes, not their noses.

Calculating each other's self-assurance is an inborn instinct that developed thousands of years ago. Imagine two club-carrying cavemen, Thag and Atouk, stumbling across each other in the wilderness. They freeze. They lock eyes. Now it's instant decision time. Is he friend or foe? If staring turns to fighting, who will win? They ask themselves . . .

"Does big Thag look powerful enough to hammer me?"

"Does little Atouk look cunning enough to outfox me?"

In a flash, each decides, "Should I fight or take flight?"

Fast-forward to today. When two competing job candidates, Carla and Conner, wait in the foyer, they don't measure each other's muscles; they instinctively calculate each other's demeanor:

"Does he look confident about getting the job?"

"Does she seem sure she'll win the desired position?"

Carla and Conner are playing professional poker—who will get the ace, and who will draw a deuce?

Once hired, exuding confidence—especially during the first several days on the job—is equally important, because bosses, supervisors, and coworkers keep a close eye on you. While shaking hands or saying hi, the caveman instinct takes over. They assess you in terms of qualities related to professional success at the company:

> "Does he look like he can handle the job?"

> "Does she look like she'll be a good asset to the team?"

> "Will he be able to relate to customers?"

> "Will she be fun to work with?"

> "Will he want my job?"

> "Will she support my project?"

They all know . . .

- A slouch can signal insecurity.

- Averted eyes may indicate timidity.

- A lowered head could mean embarrassment.

- Fidgeting might imply dishonesty.

- Folded arms could suggest defensiveness.

- Shallow breathing signals self-doubt.

Now here comes the sticky part. If they sense you're not sure of yourself, they go on heightened alert for any shortcomings. People are subject to a phenomenon scientists call "the confirmation bias," the desire to prove to themselves that their initial observations were correct. Individuals come to an almost instantaneous conclusion about you, and their inner jury quickly decides whether that impression was right or wrong. Nobody wants to feel wrong!

How many people do you think make up that jury? Not the usual twelve like American jurisprudence decrees—just one. Not only that, but this one-person jury is also the final judge. Plus he or she plays private investigator, actively searching for evidence to back up his or her initial pronouncement on you. Sadly, it doesn't take long for colleagues to *assume* they have all the answers about you.

When average employees meet you, they see you as a new colleague (aka "competitor") whom they fear might someday take their job, and so they don't want to find strong qualities; finding faults in you makes them feel more secure. Regrettably, many talented people who have the smarts to rise to the top still haven't mastered the skill of projecting self-assurance.

What about you? You know you have the insight, intelligence, ability, and talent to do the job better than anyone else, but maybe you lack the knack for showing how good you are. It's probably because nobody ever taught you the specific techniques for displaying confidence that we'll talk about here. It doesn't matter whether you've been on the job for 10 minutes, 10 years, or more; you can start using the next little trick the moment you walk in the door first thing tomorrow morning.

2

Your First Move

No doubt you've heard the expression, "You never have a second chance to make a good first impression"? Sure you have, probably so many times you'd rather eat hairballs than hear it again. The mental snapshot people take when meeting you for the first time burns itself into their memory bank and colors their opinion of you from that moment forward. And today, that first impression is more important than any time in history because people who work together in a digital world see each other far fewer times.

However, here's a little secret most people don't know. The first glimpse colleagues have of you coming in the door each morning also packs a powerful punch and has a ripple effect throughout the entire day. If your demeanor impresses colleagues and bosses at first sight that day, it becomes the image they remember and colors all subsequent interactions.

Not giving any thought to their entrance, many employees stroll into the office, thinking, "Ho hum, here I am at work again. Another day, another dollar." But suppose tomorrow a colleague shows up looking a little different, say with a new haircut. You'd spot it immediately. When you see her later in the day, you still notice the new look. The third time, however, the hairstyle is just part of her everyday image, and you're not even aware of it the next day.

Now let's talk about how you look walking into the office. Like most people, you may be ruminating about the e-mails in your inbox or stewing about something your supervisor said to you the day before. Perhaps you're figuring how to handle an upcoming videoconference with a difficult client. Maybe your mind isn't on work at all. You might be mulling over the squabble you had with your spouse last night or how the kids slammed the door when they left for school this morning. Frustrations like those can disturb your thoughts to such an extent that you're completely unaware of the image you're projecting.

You don't think other people can read your mind? In a way, they can. *Everything* shows in your expression, how you hold yourself, the way you walk, and your first words. The second they spot you, people subconsciously pick up on your vibes, and that first daily impression sticks. In a study called "First Impressions: Making up Your Mind After a 100-Ms Exposure to a Face," subjects viewed various people and recorded their immediate judgments. Even after viewing them longer, nothing significantly altered their opinions. That first flash had said it all.

Let's say you're a bit late to work because the traffic was terrible and you're frazzled. You race into the building clutching a file of papers while juggling a full cup of coffee. You fumble in your pocket or purse for your swipe card to enter. Somehow you manage to open the door without spilling or dropping anything and you barrel through.

Wait! Stop! Rewind the video a few seconds. Now take a deep breath and throw your shoulders back. Chuck your coffee cup and organize whatever you are carrying so no papers or other items are jutting out. Put on a pleasant, professional, almost serene expression. Flush any negativity out of your mind concerning coworkers you're about to see. Of course it's challenging to set aside their previous slights, dismissive attitudes, and rudeness. But if you're ruminating about the time Candice cut you off in a meeting or Curt took credit for your work, it shows. The only thing colleagues see is an employee who is stressed out or stewing about something. Turn your arrival at work into a grand entrance, like you're walking on the red carpet to accept your Oscar. It's showtime!

★ LITTLE TRICK #1

Your Daily Grand Entrance

Even if it means getting up a few minutes earlier, do all grooming before leaving home. No putting on lipstick in the rearview mirror or combing your hair as you sprint down the hall. If you're late and papers are flying out of your bag, come to a screeching halt several feet before the door. Breathe deeply and think about a song you like, your adorable pet, or that ecstatic moment on the beach. Anything but the hassles at work. Now gracefully glide in with a smile and a cheery "Good morning."

You may find it strange that a book entitled *How to Talk to Anyone at Work* begins with a technique that involves no words. Why did I do it? Because, far more than words, what your colleagues and bosses *see* has a greater impact. Many people think spoken words are the foremost way human beings communicate. This is far from the truth. The findings of Albert Mehrabian, professor emeritus of psychology at UCLA, are now universally accepted. Only 7 percent of your communication is composed of spoken words. The sound of your voice is another 38 percent. But 55 percent of your impact on your coworkers comes from your stature, your movements, and your expressions. Companies are investing billions in technology to capture these elements in robots and holograms. Will they succeed? It's too early to tell but, for now, it doesn't cost anything to let your body do a lot of the talking.

Of course, the first words out of your mouth also count, and neuroscience has shown how special it is to hear your name on someone else's lips. Studies using fMRI (functional magnetic resonance imaging) show that it activates the pleasure center in your brain. It's one of the first words a baby recognizes, so it's understandable. Since birth, your colleagues have heard their names said thousands of times by friends and loving relatives, and you saying it tomorrow morning echoes that fondness. Make it a point to greet several of your colleagues by name. Just don't overdo it, or it sounds obsequious!

Now let's talk about how to reinforce that confident and charismatic image throughout the day.

3

How to Look Dynamic All Day Long

This one makes you look like "a woman who knows where she's going" or "a man who knows what he wants." Let me tell you how this little trick was hatched. One of my speaking clients, a mergers and acquisitions (M&A) advisory firm, booked my presentation on executive image. I wasn't very familiar with M&A at the time, so before presenting to the employees, I wanted to learn more about the company's complicated business. My speakers bureau arranged for me to meet with the company's president, Peter Druss. I'm sure my first question made it blatantly obvious to him that I knew little about his field. But looking back, I'm thrilled I asked it, because his unforgettable answer gave me a big gift, the technique I'll share with you now.

My first naive query was, "Mr. Druss, how do you judge whether a company would be a good one for your client to acquire?"

"Well, it's a long process, Leil," he responded, "but my MO is always the same. First, I arrange with the company's top people to let me 'spy on' their corporate offices. By that I mean just walk around unaccompanied by any of their higher executives. Then I watch the employees going about their business, sitting at their desks in front of their computers, speaking with each other or on the phone, and doing what they usually do. I just want to observe."

"Observe what?" I asked.

"Everything! Like seeing if employees are making eye contact with each other. Are they speaking energetically among themselves at regular volume? Or are they glancing around and lowering their voices like they're afraid someone might overhear? Does there seem to be any animosity between them? Does their body language express enthusiasm, or do they look lethargic?

"And here's an observation you might find interesting, Leil. I keep my eyes open to judge their energy level and how briskly they walk, particularly when they're in the hallways or going from place to place. I watch to see if they have what I call a 'sense of destination.'"

Peter must have seen my confused expression, because he continued, "I've noticed when workers are fully productive and absorbed in their tasks, they don't amble. When they leave their desk or station, they look like they know exactly where they're going. They don't dawdle, get distracted, or check their phones for personal messages. If they pass colleagues in the hall, they might greet each other or even stop for a few words, but as they continue, their speed and sense of direction tells me a lot. Are they concentrating on the task at hand and wanting to get it done? Or are they dreading it or bored?"

As he spoke, my mind drifted to my own actions when I'm at home working on a book. I realized he was right. When I'm really into what I'm writing and get thirsty, I almost run to the kitchen for a glass of water and race back to my computer. Sometimes I'm so into it, I even find myself postponing a trip to the bathroom.

But then, when writer's block sets in as it inevitably does, I'll take the long route to the bathroom. I'll check to see if my phone is charged and then spend a few minutes in front of the mirror combing my hair or primping myself for no one. I'll mosey back to my computer by way of the kitchen to check what's in the fridge, stop in the bedroom to see if I've left my purse there, open the front door to check the weather, and then slump back to my computer.

Peter's insight into people's pace enthralled me so, while consulting at various companies in the following months, I watched the speed and energy with which everyone walked. At the more successful companies, I noticed the senior executives, both male and female, walked more directly at a faster pace.

At one longtime client's firm, management had given me a heads-up about which employees were being considered for promotions. After learning Peter Druss's method for judging a company, my observations confirmed it. I noticed the well-regarded workers walked more spritely than the others. As they went from one place to the next, they seemed to have a destination in mind and appeared to be thinking about what they had to accomplish when they arrived. Other employees walked more leisurely, almost as though they had nowhere to go. Some looked like they were searching for an excuse not to return to their desks!

Of course, this raises the question of whether certain employees were promoted because they looked determined as they walked? Or were they truly dedicated and rushing to get things done? Who knows, but the faster-walking employees were usually the ones that management had singled out for promotions. When you have a sprightly walk and definite destination in mind, everyone thinks you're more involved in your work.

Visualize yourself going from place to place on the job. Did you ever consider that even the speed of your journey to the photocopy machine could send signals about your interest in your work? If you shuffle to the supply room or the bathroom at a snail's pace, onlookers might mistakenly think you have nothing better to do, or draw the conclusion that you aren't interested in getting back to what you're being paid for.

"I Know Where I'm Going" Gait

Don't take the chance that your boss will get the wrong idea because your pace is slow. Take long brisk strides wherever you walk at work and look like you have a mission to accomplish. Keep your destination in mind, and concentrate on what you will do when you get there. Look directed. Look determined. Look dynamic!

Big Thinkers Move Big

When people tell you, "You gotta think big," they're usually referring to inspiring concepts like "visualizing impossible achievements" or "having no limits on your thinking." It's spot-on advice for anyone, and for a company owner or CEO, it can be a matter of the business's life or death. If a leader makes one damaging decision, the company can crash like a cracked glacier collapsing into the ocean. But wherever you are on the totem pole, thinking big is crucial. For the moment, however, I'd like to talk about another form of *big*. And that's the way your body moves. Big movements hint at big thoughts and complete confidence.

Some years ago, a copywriter in a California advertising agency e-mailed me, wanting coaching in communication skills. However, Livia lived too far away for me to work with her. I always tell prospective clients my coaching can't be effective unless I work with them in person. Livia's entreaty, however, was so heartfelt and sensitively written that I wanted to do what I could to help her and invited her to phone me.

When she called, her voice pleasantly surprised me. Unlike many people seeking coaching, her voice was full of vitality. She sounded like a top pro who really knew her stuff! This confused me. Why was she seeking help when her communication skills seemed excellent? She sounded vivacious, tactful, insightful, and she seemed to have all the right qualities for success. Yet she told me, "The creative director at the agency promoted copy editors who've been there less time than I have, and I truly believe their work isn't as inspired."

Now I was curious and told her that if she ever came to New York, I'd like to have lunch with her at no charge. She had a business trip planned the following month so we made a date. I arrived at the restaurant early and waited just inside. When I saw Livia, her professional attire impressed me, and she was even more attractive than her online picture. I greeted her with a warm handshake but was disappointed to feel hers was limp. She took off her coat and, with small movements, gave it to the coat-check person almost apologetically. Following me to the table, she seemed stiff and kept her hands folded neatly in her lap and her elbows close to her sides when reaching for her napkin. It seemed like she was trying to make herself as small as possible.

Although her voice was as vibrant as it had been on the phone when speaking, she looked down at the tablecloth as though she was inspecting it. At one point, Livia rested one hand on the table with her palm facing down. (Open palms suggest warmth and openness.) Her posture was exceptional but rigid. (Stiff body positions suggest rigidity of thought.) Her body leaned neither forward nor back. (Leaning toward someone while speaking expresses interest and enthusiasm. Leaning back implies the opposite.) Once or twice Livia folded her arms across her chest as though she were cold, but the restaurant was well heated. (Crossed arms can look defensive, even defiant.) While talking, she occasionally rubbed one of her arms. (This is a self-comforting motion, like caressing yourself when you're nervous.) Another time when I was speaking, she touched her ear. (This hints at not wanting to hear what's being said.)

I began to sense why Livia wasn't as respected as she deserved to be at work. No matter how effective people are in their jobs, organizations don't want them in a position of power if they come across as tentative or unsure of themselves. Unfortunately, with her small, hesitant gestures, Livia didn't look like leadership material. I now suspected why top management hadn't promoted her, because I, too, couldn't see her dynamically leading a team.

Successful people, especially effective top leaders, use wide, spread-out gestures. They walk dead center through double doors, not to one side. They reach for things faster, not hesitantly, and use more massive movements than less self-assured employees. In other words, they use their entire personal space.

What is personal space? You've seen kids blowing those sudsy bubbles out of wands? Well, imagine one of those invisible globes encapsulating you. Employees who are less confident crouch in the middle of theirs, trying to make themselves as small as possible, almost as though they don't want to be seen. But those who are sure of themselves fill their entire bubble to the max. Whether sitting or standing, they put themselves in a power position taking up the entire bubble "they own."

This instinct comes naturally to all primates. When a gorilla strives to show he's king of the jungle, he stands upright, making himself taller. He widens his shoulders, thrusts his chest, and spreads his legs as if to say, "Look at me! Me big. Me powerful. Me strong." He might even beat his chest and follow it with a bloodcurdling bellow. Fortunately, human beings aren't that obvious. (Well, most of them at least.) Noticeable changes do, however, take place in every employee's body when he or she feels powerful, capable, and confident. Everything expands.

How can you train yourself to make bigger movements second nature? Like any physical habit, it's a matter of consciousness and practice. As far-fetched as it sounds, the following technique works.

LITTLE TRICK #3

Make Your Bubble Bigger

As soon as you get out of bed in the morning, stand up straight, clasp and interlock both hands over your head, and stretch your body to the right and to the left. Then extend your arms to their full length and swing them around in big circles. Roll your hips, kick your legs, and punch the air. Feel every inch of the big invisible bubble surrounding you and know it's all yours. Taking up more personal space puts you in a confident mindset to meet the rest of your challenges that day.

Doing this drill just once in the morning, however, isn't enough. Find a place at work where no one can see you, perhaps an empty office or hallway, the supply room, or outdoors behind the building. I especially suggest this exercise before attending a significant meeting, having a performance review, meeting a new customer, or confronting any stressful situation. I do it before every speech I give, even though sometimes the only private space I can find at the venue is a bathroom stall. Think of it as a warm-up for success!

Calculate Your Coworkers' Confidence

Having met and subsequently worked with thousands of people, I've learned to spot their confidence or lack thereof right off the bat. My antenna now picks up on how self-assured an individual is. You may not have considered it before, but you'd be surprised how much clout it gives you to know your colleagues' and boss's confidence level. That sensitivity will help guide your strategy in subsequent interactions. For instance, you'd deal quite differently with someone who has small ideas and a big ego versus someone who has big ideas and a small ego. Also gauging your boss's self-assurance level helps you handle her more strategically. Evaluating everyone's confidence is yet another instrument to add to your communication skills toolkit. When you watch how your colleagues move, you'll probably spot lack of self-assurance all around you—which should give you more!

5

You Are So Much More Than Your Job Description

Let me ask you a question that I'm sure you've been asked hundreds of times. "What do you do?" Before answering that, stop! I hope you weren't just going to give me just your job title. You are so much more than that and far exceed what the company has decreed should be on your business card.

People usually think of networking as something they do outside their job, particularly when looking for a new one or meeting other professionals in the same field. However, I haven't often heard employees talking about networking *inside* their own companies, which is just as vital to success. While chatting with someone you haven't met at the company's holiday party, delivering an envelope to a different department, or talking with an employee you don't know in the elevator, the person will no doubt ask, "What do you do here?"

It's the common question I ask people at the various companies where I consult. At one of them, spotting an employee sitting alone in the lunchroom, I asked if I could join her. "Of course," she answered graciously, "please do." I then asked her what she did there. The young lady smiled and said, "I'm just the receptionist."

I wanted to shake her! Why did she demean herself by saying, "just"? Did she really think her job was that unimportant? Didn't she realize that she was the first person that people saw the moment they entered the company? In a sense, she was the gateway to the organization. She was probably hired because of the same type of friendliness she'd displayed to me. It's a special quality, and the poor girl actually saw her crucial position as insignificant. "No, you are not *just* the receptionist," I gently chided her with a smile. "You are *the* receptionist." After a nervous laugh, she looked at me as though I were a little strange.

Saying "I'm *just* the . . ." anything is self-deprecating and makes you sound like you're embarrassed by your job. How much more impressive the receptionist would have been if she'd enthusiastically fleshed out her job description and perhaps told me some of her duties.

Networking Is an Inside Job, Too

Talking about your job in an upbeat manner makes you more memorable inside your company if other opportunities crop up. Think of it as the "elevator speech" that all top professionals give, a brief description or "commercial" about what they do. Get your name around *inside* your organization.

Don't just give your official title when coworkers you don't know ask you what you do there. You perform certain duties at your company that enhance the bottom line, otherwise, you wouldn't be there. Tell them about those. Just saying, "office manager," "assistant sales manager," or "travel coordinator" isn't memorable. Say more. Depending on how familiar the person is with your department, flesh it out for them.

For example, instead of presenting a confining job title like "office manager," try something like "I liaise with staff and suppliers, handle purchasing, and attend meetings with senior management"—and sound excited about it! Instead of saying "I'm the assistant sales manager," how about "I help construct the sales plans, set quotas, and analyze data for the sales department." Rather than "I'm the travel coordinator," say "I make domestic and international transportation and lodging arrangements for the entire company." Be sure to talk about whatever you do with gusto and vitality, because expressing enthusiasm about your work is vital for professional success.

Your In-House Elevator Speech

Starting today, put "meeting coworkers in other departments" on your daily to-do list. When people you haven't met in the company ask what you do, give them a short description and sound upbeat. Sure, you can include your official title, but make that just a part of the answer, maybe at the end. When departments are discussing promotions and who they can nab from other departments, you want your name to come to mind.

6

What's Your
On-the-Job Face?

Whether you've been top dog at your company for 20 years or are the new pup who started yesterday, this seldom discussed little trick makes you look confident and in control even when you think no one is watching.

Few employees ever think about it, but just like you have a "resting heart rate," you have a "resting facial expression." Some workers' lips naturally curve up at the edges, and those blessed with that upward tilt look more approachable and at peace with themselves. Other people's lips curve slightly down, which, unfortunately, can give off an unintended impression of unrest or irritation. You could be the warmest, most tranquil person in the company, but if God gave you downward-tilting lips, your coworkers might see you as otherwise. Most babies aren't born with tightened lips or a grumpy expression, but it can result from a rough childhood or years of negative experiences. The good news is that a troubled or insecure expression needn't be permanent. It just means those folks must consciously work on changing it.

If you're on the job right now, look around at your coworkers and you'll see the tips of everyone's lips curl slightly up or down. If you're curious about your resting facial expression, take a mirror, close your eyes, and push all thoughts out of your head. Now open them quickly and look at your lips. If the corners of your mouth slope slightly up, you are one of the lucky minority. I know it sounds touchy-feely, but I sometimes tell students in my classes to close their eyes and picture someone they love. Or perhaps think about their pet or favorite vacation place. Even an activity they look forward to or any private thought that gives them pleasure. While they have their eyes closed, I scan the crowd. During those moments, I see a remarkable change slowly sweep over their faces. Tension, aloofness, and nervousness fade. Serenity replaces it. I now feel I'm looking at a confident and content group of people.

As I said, some are fortunate to be born with that calm, cheerful look on their faces at rest, and others must work at it like I did. After consciously using the following little trick for about a month, I found that a pleasant expression is now habitual. This peaceful look improves how everyone responds to you at work.

LITTLE TRICK #5

The Serenity Semi-Smile

When you're not directly communicating with each other (which is more than 90 percent of the time), coworkers still get an impression of you. Make an effort to softly lift the corners of your mouth even when you think no one is looking your way. It's not really a smile, just a serene and peaceful expression. You might put a reminder on your desk. Photos of your kids or a loved one would be a good choice to give you that "sliver of a smile." But, hey, whatever works for you.

An additional self-check is to feel whether your shoulders are tight or perhaps pulled slightly up toward your ears. If so, relax them because that's another sign of tension.

Next let's talk about the most important indicator of your confidence or lack of it. The following is like a 24-hour broadcasting station showing anyone within eyeshot precisely how you feel about yourself at any particular moment.

7

Your Biggest
Confidence Barometer

Imagine yourself all alone at home in front of the TV while the winning lottery numbers are being announced. The first two numbers sound like they might be yours so your ears perk up. You scramble through your pockets to confrm it. They are, and OMG, the next few are yours, too. By now, the wrinkled receipt clutched in your sweaty hands is soaked. And when the final number is called, you realize you've won the lottery! Your head jolts up and your shoulders shoot back without your even thinking about it. Your entire body radiates energy because you are a winner! Now there's a spring in your step, vitality in your eyes, and a soft smile frames your lips for the rest of the week. Your body language screams "success." That's the image you want at work!

Over the years, friends and family have taken hundreds of snapshots of you on their phones. In most of them, you're smiling and standing tall because you're usually enjoying yourself. Your brow isn't furrowed, your shoulders aren't hunched, and you don't look worried or anxious. But what does your body broadcast about you at work? If someone secretly snapped a shot of you sitting at your desk, dealing with a customer, or having a coffee in the break room, what would the photo show? Do you look like a winner? Or would the lens find you slumped over papers at your desk, slouched at the counter, or leaning against the wall? Perhaps it was just for a few minutes, but it only takes a split second for anyone looking your way to form an impression. You may seldom be in those positions, but suppose your boss happened to walk by at an ill-timed moment? Spotting you like that enough times could give the impression you're a sluggish worker.

Good posture is vital to your image which, in turn, stimulates confidence. Harvard University and Columbia University researchers proved the symbiotic relationship in a study called "Do Slumped and Upright Postures Affect Stress Responses?" They first told 26 women and 16 men to spit into a test tube for saliva samples, and then directed them to sit in slouched positions. "Hold your elbows close to your body, drop your head, and hold a scrunched-up position for two full minutes." At that point they took a second saliva sample.

After squirreling the samples away, the researchers instructed the subjects to now stand up straight, throw their heads back, thrust their chests out, rest their shoulders, and take up a lot of space for the next two minutes. Afterward, another saliva sample. The results? The researchers discovered a dramatic difference in the subjects' testosterone and cortisone levels. After sitting in upright positions, their testosterone (the hormone that signifies feeling strong and more willing to take risks in both females and males) shot up, and their cortisol (the hormone that makes us susceptible to stress) shrank. Conversely, after the low-power pose, the subjects' cortisol level jumped and their testosterone took a five-point nose dive. It's proof that excellent posture doesn't just make you look better; you feel more confident, think more clearly, and make better judgments.

So how do you make perfect posture natural? No, it's not by going to the gym twice a week (although that helps) or balancing a book on your head. To make it your natural position, you must practice it—a lot. That means while walking down the hall, sitting at your computer, or chatting with colleagues. It means when driving the car, having dinner with the family, or enjoying a beer with friends. Perfect alignment must become second nature so you don't even need to think about it. But to achieve that, you need a constant reminder. Unfortunately you can't hire a physical trainer to follow you around at work.

Here's a solution: Think of something you normally do many times each day and make that your cue. For instance, you're constantly walking through doorways—morning, afternoon and night. You enter and leave your company building and go through dozens of office doors daily. You enter and exit the restroom, the break room, and places where you eat. At home there's the front door, kitchen door, living room door, bedroom door, and more. One day I decided to count how many doors I walked through. It came to 50! And I bet many of you busy folks top that.

Doorway to Confidence

Let every door you walk through remind you to lift your head higher (as though you wanted your hair to brush the top of the doorway.) And throw out your chest (as though you wanted it to go through first.) This technique is especially important entering the conference room, your boss's office, and everywhere else you want to make a great impression. Turn every doorway into your free physical trainer nudging you to stand taller. Before long, it becomes natural to look like a winner at all times.

8

A Crafty Way to Calculate Their Confidence—and Convince Them of Yours

On your way to the top, it's important to know how sure of themselves the people you work with are so you can deal with them more effectively. This next little trick gives you rare insight into that.

You've fed pigeons in the park, right? After tossing a few breadcrumbs on the ground, hungry little birds magically appear from nowhere and apprehensively land about 10 feet away. In time, one brave bird bolts at a crumb, grabs it in his beak, and makes a quick getaway. His fellow pigeons, pleased to see their bold feathered friend survived, follow suit and scurry toward the crumbs. As they become confident that you won't hurt them, they come even closer, and soon you're surrounded by a flock of pigeons.

Human beings have pigeon instincts, too. When a coworker feels confident and comfortable with you—let's just say she feels "safe"—she'll move physically closer. But if she feels inferior or harbors negative feelings toward you, she'll stand farther away. You unconsciously do the same. Say you're a woman talking to another woman with whom you've been working a long time. As the conversation develops, you instinctively come closer because you feel comfortable with her. If you also happen to be friends outside the office, you move even nearer. Conversely, if you find her intimidating, you step back without even thinking about it.

Distance reveals a lot. A meek employee might tap lightly on the boss's door, take a few tentative steps into that "scary territory," and ask a question hovering close to the door. But your boss might march into your space and come right up to your desk. Here's where the science of human distances called "proxemics" comes into play The good news is that you can learn this subtle skill of maintaining strategic distances to project the image you want.

The specifics vary by culture, but for North America, I turn to anthropologist Edward Hall, who divided the measurements into "Intimate Distance, "Personal Distance," "Social Distance," and "Public Distance." Unfortunately, knowing his calculations in feet and inches isn't practical for me. I just can't wrap my head around gauging distances in space. And I'm not about to take out a tape measure, put one end on the tip of a colleague's nose, and pull the other back to mine. So let me share my method with you because insight into workplace relationship subtleties gives you a big advantage.

Imagine yourself standing and speaking with a colleague, and you both put your arms straight out in front of you. If the tips of your middle fingers are still inches apart, it might indicate one of you finds the other intimidating or there's antagonism. I call this the "No Fingertip Touch." To express more warm confidence, step forward so the palms of your hands can lie flat against each other's. I label this the "Full Palm Press."

To appear completely confident, casual, and comfortable with someone, envision both of you with arms straight forward, grasping each other's wrists or even forearms. Gentlemen, since it's natural for you to stand farther away from another man, you might find this "Wrist or Forearm Grasp" a little creepy. Follow your instincts, and to be on the safe side, put the same distance between you and a female colleague as you would if you were talking to another man. If she steps closer, that's her choice, but beware, it could send the wrong message to onlookers.

There's a final distance category, but it's way too close for comfort at work. I call that the "Nose Tip Touch," where your finger can touch the tip of your colleague's nose. No matter how friendly you two are, avoid this one on the job!

Proxemics may sound like minutia or even plain nonsense to you, but I promise, the distance between you signals a lot.

Come Confidently Closer

Shrinking your distance from someone shows you feel sure of yourself. Stepping closer is an excellent way to mask insecurity or hostility, so, any time anyone at work intimidates or irritates you, just smile slightly and step a tad closer. They'll never know you're afraid or angry.

However, here is a big *don't*. If a coworker adjusts the distance between you by moving back, do not step closer, because that's encroaching on her space. And of course, if she steps nearer to you, hold your ground. That's *her* comfort zone. Everyone's is different.

In business, it's not only strategic to gauge a colleague's confidence level, it's also helps to know his opinion on your ideas even if he's silent. His distance choice is a clue to both. Emma, a supervisor in one of my classes, said that, after giving her team members an assignment, she watches carefully to determine if their heads inch subconsciously toward her or away. "Knowing how they feel about a certain situation," she said, "helps me work with various employees throughout the project." The following tip helps determine how your coworkers feel about you and what you're saying at the moment. This knowledge can be important in your future interactions with them.

Examine *Their* Distance Choice

If you want to know a coworker's sentiments about you or your words, take note of that individual's habitual stance when talking with others. Then compare it with how close he or she chooses to be to you. Believe it or not, being sensitive to nuances like this can help you circumvent negative workplace relationships.

9

How to Sound Self-Assured in E-mail and IM

Since so much communication (the majority of it in many companies) is e-mail and instant messaging, let's talk about coming across as confident in writing, too. Unfortunately, impressive entrances, walking energetically, making larger movements, maintaining a peaceful self-assured expression, standing or sitting tall, and coming a tad closer don't work in writing. So, how do you sound more confident in your e-mail?

For the answer, let's go back to a kids' game many of us played in our coloring books called "What's Wrong with This Picture?" You may remember it. You'd find funny drawings of stuff—like a farm with animals grazing, a tractor, a couple of flags to show the directions of the wind, and lots more. Most of the objects in the sketch looked normal, but the instructions told you to circle any mistakes. So you dutifully took a big crayon out of the box and got to work. You were a keen-eyed kid and you saw the tractor had only three wheels. Great, you circled it. You searched around a little more and then, aha, there were two flags blowing in opposite directions. You circled those, too. Now you were on a roll. You also marked the dog who had a cat's head and the barefoot kid with six toes and lots more "wrong stuff."

Now let's play a grown-up version of "What's Wrong with This Picture?" called "What's Wrong with This Sentence?" (Don't worry; I haven't cracked up. It leads to a technique to make you sound more confident online.) Here are some sentences that people have e-mailed me. Mark any of them in which the senders sound less sure of themselves.

> Serena wrote: "I wanted to know if the conference is still scheduled."

> Tomás wrote, "I'll try to get it done today."

> Clarissa wrote: "I think we should send it to the client next week."

> Mackenzie wrote: "I'm sorry I can't make the meeting today. Would tomorrow work for you?"

> Judah wrote, "I just want to ask if you received it."

Which sentences made the writer sound insecure? I'm sure you've guessed the answer. *All* of them. Why? Their messages included what I call "Weakening Words."

Serena, don't you still want to know if the conference is on schedule? Putting your desires in the past tense is one of the most prevalent examples of "humble writing." Far too often people have sent me self-deprecating sentences like "I was hoping you would have time to talk about it" or "I wanted to ask your opinion." Putting your desires in the past makes you sound like you're embarrassed about them. Put your wishes in the fearless present, which confidently says what you mean, "Here's what I want *now*."

Tomás, the word "try" always sounds weak—like you're not sure you can accomplish what you want to do. "I will get it done this week barring any big obstacles" shows you have more assurance in your abilities.

Clarissa, you "*think*" we should send it to the client next week? You'd sound stronger saying, "My suggestion is . . ." or "My position is . . ."

Mackenzie, why are you apologizing? You're not doing anything wrong. Simply write, "I regret I can't make the meeting today" and then ask about your recipient's availability tomorrow.

Judah, of course you want to know if the person you're writing to received the order, and you have every right to know. "Just ask, "Have you received the order?" You'll sound surer of yourself.

The list of weak phrases to drop goes on— "This is "just a thought," or "just a question," "Sorry to bother you," "I might," "I can't," "sort of," "I'm wondering if." Well, you get the idea. Substitute all of them with something stronger.

★ LITTLE TRICK #9

Avoid Weakening Words

Avoid common phrases like "I'll try," "I think," "I just" and the others we talked about. Also steer clear of the self-belittling much overused past tense for something you still want or feel. Above all, there's no need to say "I'm sorry" when you're not guilty of anything. (We women do that far too often!)

10

Can You Look Too Confident?

As I reflect on the hundreds of speeches and seminars I've given over the years, several stand out for different reasons. I especially remember this next one because of the amazing audience.

A few years ago, Martin, the head of a speakers bureau I often work with, called saying the Young Presidents Organization (YPO), a prestigious group of men and women who became presidents of their companies before the age of 45, wanted me to give a breakout session at its next annual conference. I was thrilled, because fellow speakers had told me YPO members were an inspiring group. I called the bureau the next day to learn more about what they wanted. Martin said they'd asked for my most popular presentation, "How to Talk to Anyone."

"You're kidding," I laughed. "What could I possibly teach these accomplished folks about communicating? If they've become presidents or CEOs of their companies so young, they must already be super communicators."

"What can I say, Leil? Their meeting planner asked for it. Shall I accept for you or not?"

"Yes! Absolutely! Are there any particulars they want me to concentrate on?"

"They specifically asked for tips on body language," he answered.

"Whaaat?" I gasped.

"That's what they told me. I guess that means they want to know how to look even more presidential."

"Ha ha ha," I smirked

"No, I'm dead serious."

Then grasping at straws, I said, "Well, maybe some of them want it because they inherited the company, married into it, or were somehow related to the founders." Martin shrugged. (Incidentally, I discovered I was dead wrong about that. With few exceptions, YPO members had reached their heights the old-fashioned way, earning it through hard work, making the right decisions, and looking like a leader.)

The day before my presentation, I flew to Colorado Springs. As I entered the huge hotel lobby, attendees were having lively chats with one another as they were signing in. Glancing around the group, it struck me how states-manlike and completely sure of themselves they all looked. Riding up in the elevator to my room, I felt like a 10-year-

old hired to teach brain surgeons how to perform a crani-
otomy and feared whoever booked me would get canned
from the speaker search committee. The organizer had
scheduled my session for 9 a.m. the next day. "Well, that's
good," I figured, "because most of them will be sleeping in
after their long trips and the welcome party that went on
past midnight."

No such luck! At 9 a.m. sharp, the room was packed
with a crowd of about 60 men and women looking very presidential indeed. I was thoroughly convinced my content
would be too basic and pictured them walking out the door,
one by one or in small groups, leaving me stranded in a huge
empty room.

The Surprise Ending

Much to my surprise, my presentation became the most
talked about session of the weekend! I opened by commend-
ing them on their commanding look of leadership. Then it
was sheer dumb luck that I happened to joke, "What could I
possibly teach you?" At that, one attendee cupped his hands
around his lips and called out, "How to tone it down!" They
all laughed. But he was dead serious; that's what they wanted!
When I asked why, several told me they'd been accused of
having a "superior attitude" at their companies. One said
he'd heard his employees thought he was "insensitive."
Another said she was accused of being "inattentive." Now I

got really psyched and turned my planned presentation into an open discussion.

One president in the audience explained that the members were well aware of this problem in previous years and had booked presentations on what leaders could *say* to employees to sound friendlier. But apparently, various complaints at their companies continued. That year, the member responsible for finding a speaker was a woman who had another theory. Being familiar with her colleagues at YPO, she suspected their physical demeanor might be the problem, so she asked the bureau for a body language speaker.

At that moment, I retroactively forgave Martin for not having understood his client's needs better. It wasn't his fault, because it certainly was a one-of-a-kind request. No meeting planner had ever asked for a program on how to *not* look so sure of yourself! As the presidents offered their testimonies, the cacophony of complaints about bosses in my seminars resounded in my ears. I told the group what many of my students had grumbled:

> "My boss points her finger right at me when accusing me of something."

> "Mine squints at me like he doesn't believe a word I'm saying."

> "When I'm talking to him, he crosses his arms in front of his chest."

"She stands with her hands on her hips and gives me directions."

"He turns away while I'm trying to explain something to him."

I saw a few sheepish smiles around the room as I mentioned various complaints. A few even playfully mumbled, "Guilty." At that point, I also spotted a couple of confused expressions. One woman had been nervously rubbing the back of her neck and stroking her forearm. Since the session had become more of an open discussion than a presentation, I asked her thoughts on the subject. She looked around and said, "Well, as some of you know, my company is a family business which I took over when my dad died last year. I know the field inside out, having grown up with it, but I never felt secure being in this leadership position, so I guess sometimes I overdo it." Several other young presidents in the room nodded empathetically. I sensed she wasn't the only one who used bold gestures to cover up a basic insecurity.

She noticed there was a pad of paper on an easel in the room and offered to write down some of the arrogant gestures we'd been discussing, and as I handed her the magic marker, the others clapped.

The session was lively to say the least; by the end, she'd written six full pages of employee complaints. It was an unforgettable afternoon for me. After the session, I snatched the sheets off the pad, took them up to my room, and packed them in my suitcase. Here are some selections from those sheets:

"My boss leans back and crosses his arms when I'm talking, like I'm a nobody."

"She walks right past me when she sees me in the hall."

"He doodles on his pad when I'm making a presentation in a meeting."

"She hangs over my desk like she's so superior."

"When I'm trying to tell him something, he sometimes puts his feet up on the desk."

"While I'm talking to her in her office, she looks at her computer every time she hears a new e-mail coming in."

"He leans back and puts his arms behind his head with his elbows jutting out."

"She waves her finger like a metronome when she disagrees with what I've said."

"He leans over my desk, putting his palms down on it, and stares at me."

"She puts her chin in the air and looks down her nose at me."

Gestures That Shout, "I'm Better Than You"

We saw that the list on the easel fell into three categories:

- **Acting superior.** Putting their hands on their hips, leaning back with arms behind their head, putting feet up on their desks, and steepling their hands

- **Disinterest.** Not making eye contact, looking bored, or not listening

- **Rejection.** Folding their arms, rolling their eyes, or turning away while being talked to

LITTLE TRICK #10

Stamp Out Superiority Signals

Always look in command and self-assured at work, but avoid thoughtless, overbearing gestures. Coming off as *too* cocksure of yourself can obstruct your climb up the ladder because employees resent those who act like they're better than everyone else.

Now let's talk about an equally important quality for professional success and happiness. It's caring about the people you work with, which, sadly, seems missing in many companies today. I'm sure you've heard the axiom "People don't care how much you know until they know how much you care." Truer words were never spoken, and we'll tackle that now.

PART II

CARING

11

Treat Their Ego
Like Eggshells

Hemophiliacs are people who bleed profusely when their skin is pricked. Everyone you work with has a comparable condition, but this one has nothing to do with blood or skin. They bleed emotionally when anyone punctures their ego. Let's call these folks "egophiliacs." Are they bad people? No. It simply means they are human. Deep inside everyone is a big baby rattling the crib, wanting attention and screaming to be recognized as "special." (Each *is* in his or her own way, you know.) Everyone brings a distinct set of life experience to work and each has a different self-image.

What exactly is ego? In the simplest terms, it's the narrative people create about themselves. It's who they've spent every hour of every day of their lives becoming, and so protecting their egos is, in a sense, a matter of survival. People's egos are as delicate as eggshells. You must have the talent of a blind ballet dancer prancing on a stage strewn with these fragile shells, and not breaking even one.

As you grow in your company, you'll have to make clear and decisive judgment calls for the betterment of your organization. But to be a true success, you must do it without destroying the dignity and pride of the people you work with. Often employees won't like it when you stay firm on an unpopular stance. You must correct poor performance, say no when asked for something, and sometimes fire people you personally like. Those are just a few of the stairs you'll climb on the way to the top. But if you develop the professional dexterity to achieve those goals while making people feel good about themselves and their capabilities, you've really made it and deserve to be at the top. Now let's talk about how to do that, and we'll start with your smile.

12

Is the Sincere Smile an
Oxymoron at Work?

People smile at work—sometimes even sincerely! I'm sure you've seen many other types of smiles around the office, too. Smiles of surrender, smiles of deception, phony smiles, lecherous smiles, and those that are just plain ludicrous. When the big boss tells a joke, I've seen employees force grins so big they look like monkeys on a banana boat. Don't people realize a smile is a lot more than flashing teeth, parting lips, and saying cheese?

Wouldn't it be wonderful to work in a company where you didn't have to fake a smile, or for that matter, any emotions you don't feel? A company where you didn't have to pretend you thought your colleague's presentation was great or you really cared about a coworker's weekend plans? But in the hundreds of organizations I've worked with, I've yet to discover even one where employees don't sometimes need to fake smiles. Often you don't think something's funny or agree with what somebody's saying. But for tactical—or humane—reasons, you must pretend that you do.

You should also learn to recognize when your colleagues' smiles are bogus, because without that ability, you might make wrong choices and big mistakes. No doubt you've heard that a real smile reaches the eyes. When someone genuinely agrees with you, chuckles at something witty you've said, or just appreciates your ideas, you see it in the person's eyes. Or more accurately, you see it just beside their eyes in the little wrinkles around them. They're called your orbicularis oculi. (You really needed to know that, didn't you?)

"Great," you might figure, "so I'll just crinkle my eyes when I'm smiling at someone." Not so fast! That's impossible, because orbicularis oculi are involuntary muscles that you can't crinkle at will. Sincere smiles will eventually give you crow's feet, but they're well worth it.

Another huge difference between genuine and counterfeit smiles concerns the speed. When you're faking a smile, your lips jolt instantly up and you quickly flash your teeth. However, when you truly do appreciate what you're hearing or find something funny, it takes longer for the meaning of the words to sink in. Thoughtful and truthful people smile slightly more slowly because they're not faking it. They need a moment to understand what you're saying, and only then do their smiles erupt naturally. So here's the secret to making yours sincere.

LITTLE TRICK #11

The Slow Spillover Smile

Don't smile too fast! Make it just as large, but slow it down. Listen carefully to what the speaker is saying; then let a smile envelop your face and engulf the recipient like a warm wave. Think of it starting in your heart, traveling to your brain, and finally making it to your lips. We're talking milliseconds here, but it makes a huge difference. People who smile too fast look fake, and that's worse than not smiling at all.

The next little trick is for women only. (Men, you can skim, but don't forget to read the last two sentences in the paragraph that follows the technique because that tip is for you.)

Women, a Quick Smile and a Slow Jet Get You Nowhere Fast

Have you heard of confederate dollars? History buffs, you'll know the newly formed Confederacy issued them just before the outbreak of the American Civil War, but because the dollars weren't backed by anything, the value quickly dropped to a nickel or below. Likewise, sisters, if you smile too often, as many women do, the value of your smiles drops drastically. We, of the erroneously called "gentle sex," have used smiles all our lives to great advantage. Sitting on Daddy's lap when we were little, we knew that an adorable grin often got us what we wanted. Then during our teens, we discovered smiling at a guy was a great way to lure him over. And even now, when we get together with girlfriends socially, it's smiles galore. Why not? They're fun.

At work, however, you have different priorities. Your corporate colleagues, especially males, might misinterpret your smiles and misconstrue them as weakness or even flirting. Even if you are the strongest, most proficient person in the company, don't depend on smiles to get you what you want like they did with Daddy.

The Success of the Withheld Smile

Several years ago, an association of engineers hired me to give a series of communications skills presentations to their members. The vice president, Florence, with whom I'd previously had only e-mail contact, invited me to meet with her managers one morning, all males. When I arrived, Florence, a stately, subdued woman, stood up and graciously extended her hand, saying, "It's nice to see you, Leilie."

Leilie! How strange! That was my nickname in high school, which I promptly dropped on graduation day. (It didn't sound like the "serious professional woman" I aspired to be.) Oh well, I figured, it must have been a slip of the tongue. But then things got even stranger. Once during the meeting, this highly professional woman winked at me. *Weird!* Especially because she'd acted quite commanding throughout the discussions. I tried to push her wink out of my mind while we continued talking about my upcoming presentation.

As the men were leaving the conference room, Florence said, "Leilie, can you stay for a minute?" She then closed the door and giggled. I was dumbfounded because giggling was not this woman's style! Her face exploded into a wide warm smile, and she held out her arms for a hug. *Holy cow, what is this all about?* Only then did it dawn on me. I finally recognized Florence—she was from my high school (except then she was called "Flossie"). Her quicksilver smile and contagious laugh were legendary in school, and it endeared her to everyone. Flossie was an incurable giggler, and that was part of her charm. Flabbergasted, I said, "Oh my gosh! Flossie, is that you?"

"Yes, Leilie, it's so good to see you!" she squealed, giving me a hug. "If you're free, can we have lunch today?"

"Absolutely! We have so much to catch up on." What I most wanted to catch up on was why Florence seemed so super-professional at the office and then, the moment her colleagues left, she reverted to the old effervescent Flossie. Halfway through lunch, and emboldened by a glass of wine, I asked my burning question. "Uh, Florence, you seemed so different at the office . . ."

She laughed gleefully, saying, "Oh, Leilie, just call me Flossie. And there's no need to ask why I seem different. I'm not. It's just that I don't smile all the time like I used to." Her face then got serious, and she went on to explain, "Actually the only thing that's changed is how *quickly* I smile or laugh. At my old job, people far junior to me were getting promoted and I wasn't. Because engineering is a male-dominated industry, I suspected my gender was keeping me back. So I did some research on gender differences and came across tons of studies talking about how women smile much more often than men, and how that can sometimes undermine our seriousness."

"So, uh, did you stop smiling?"

"Heavens, no!" she chuckled, feigning shock. "I just changed how often I smile. Now there's a world of difference in how people at work respond to me, especially men. When I enjoy something or find it funny, of course I smile. But when I'm in a business setting, I'm a little more stingy with them. And if I don't approve of something, I don't fake one like I used to. I guess I did that when I was younger because I desperately wanted to be liked."

Flossie and I then talked about the renowned anthropologist Helen Fisher's extensive studies on human nature saying that many males often view a woman smiling as subservient, weak, and vulnerable. We laughed about how, when we were in school, men passing us on the street would sometimes say, "Hey, young lady, smile!" If they said that to a man, they'd get slugged.

I, too, had read the research and realized she had done the right thing. The proof is she'd worked her way up to vice president at her new job in a predominately male company. No quick smiles were holding Flossie back! (Nor was her nickname, which she dropped in favor of her birth name, Florence.) Too many smiles lose their value. Ladies, I suggest this modification of your smile policy.

★ LITTLE TRICK #12

Smile Amendment for Women

Especially those of you who are surrounded by men on the job, avoid your instinct of smiling too soon, too big, too often. Doling out lots of fast smiles doesn't enhance your image as a top professional. Save your lovely quick smiles for your friends, family, and the kids.

However, I'd like to add an important note for female supervisors: if you're the boss, you can be more generous with your smiles when working with reports, and it will pay off in your team's productivity big time. And, gentlemen, let your fellow employees and reports, especially the women, witness more of them. A man with a big, warm, sincere smile is a joy to work with.

Sometimes a Speedy Smile Is Essential

While I was sounding off on the "Slow Spillover Smile" and "Smile Amendment," I hope you didn't think I was disparaging the very significant "quick smile." Every smile doesn't have to be a reality show! In fact, in certain professions such as customer service, a quick smile is crucial. How many times has a gas station attendant, grocery clerk, or hotel receptionist handed you a receipt with a deadpan expression? At times I've had to bite my tongue to keep myself from blurting out, "Hey buddy, would a smile really crack your face?" Customer service without a smile is customer *dis*service.

The president of a small retail bank for which I consult was concerned about an unusually high number of customers transferring their accounts to other institutions. He told me that they'd been getting complaints about the tellers. "I don't understand it, Leil," he said. "Our tellers are highly trained and are extremely competent." The aggrieved man sounded like he was at his wit's end over it.

I started my detective work by opening a small account at his bank. I went there to deposit money or cash a check at their busiest time, lunch hour, to "spy" on the tellers while I was waiting in line. The same scene unfolded over and over. Customers approached the tellers who did their job as they were trained—checking figures, counting cash, filling in forms, and doing everything according to bank standards. To me, at least, the problem was obvious. The only thing the tellers lacked was a simple welcoming smile for each customer. When finished with one client, they'd call out, "Next," sometimes without even looking up. When it was my turn, I'd make eye contact, smile, and say, "Good morning." To which my teller would respond with a flat "G'morning" and answer my questions with a deadpan face.

Standing at the counter looking to both the right and left, I saw that other customers' transactions seemed to be going smoothly, too. But I didn't spot a smile on any of the tellers'—or the clients'—faces. At the end of each transaction, I'd hear the tellers mumble, "Have a nice day," as though it were a death threat.

After repeating this experience for the next few days with a different teller, I saw that the bank's problem was endemic. Together with the supervisors, so they could monitor their reports, I gave the tellers what we jokingly referred to as "smile training." As hackneyed as it sounds, it worked. Far fewer customer complaints came in after our smile training sessions, and the bank looked like a much happier place to be, for both tellers and customers.

★ LITTLE TRICK #13

Quick Smiles Count, Too

Especially in customer service! Sometimes there's no time or no need for you to give the slow spillover smile. For these occasions, a quick welcoming one at the beginning, a few occasional ones during, and a goodbye smile at the end of a short encounter make a world of difference. There's something in it for you, too. Customers and colleagues you barely know will treat you much better.

13

Track Them with Your Torso

Due to bitter bickering over vacation schedules at Burns and Company, a supervisor threw up her hands in exasperation and told her direct reports that this year she was just going to assign vacations. When she called the members of her team together around the conference table to announce her decisions, they were all anxious. They immediately turned full-body toward her, breathlessly awaiting their holiday fate.

"Kelsey, you have December 15 through January 1."

"*Hooray!*" Kelsey exclaims to herself, and her imagination lights up with visions of the sparkling Christmas tree she's planning. Her body leans forward toward the bearer of good news. "*Bless you!*" she's thinking.

"Aruego, you have November seventh through the thirtieth."

"*How could she do this to me?*" Aruego grouses to himself. "*That's lousy beach weather.*" He starts turning his upper body away toward the door, but stops midway, remembering, "*That's Thanksgiving. Oh well, at least we can now plan a family trip.*" He pivots halfway back toward his boss.

"Don, yours is March first through the fifteenth."

"*Dang!*" Don doesn't like that one bit. "*What a witch she is!*" He leans back, folds his arms, and turns his shoulders more toward the door.

Even if these employees had bags over their heads, you wouldn't need to be psychic to know how each of them felt about their boss at that moment. Kelsey's warmth; Aruego's disappointment; Don's anger. All were obvious because the way their upper bodies were facing was a dead giveaway. Your eyes, arms, hands, legs, and every other part of your body reveal your emotions to the discerning eye, but the direction in which your upper body turns shouts it. No clairvoyance necessary.

Sydney Patterson is probably the most beloved supervisor at one company where I consult. When conducting meetings, she never sits at the head of the long rectangular conference table. Instead, she positions herself between two employees on one of the long sides, and whenever one of her reports speaks, she pivots her head and chest in that individual's direction. She nods as she listens to each, making it clear she understands, and occasionally interjects, "That's an interesting point," "I see what you're saying," or "We'll definitely have to think about that." The only times she looks away are to briefly scribble a note on her pad about what the employee is saying, which makes each feel valued.

I also noticed that whenever she speaks to one of her employees in the hall, her body turns 100 percent toward that individual. If talking with two of them, the top of her body pivots gently from one to the other. Every single direct report feels heard and cared for, and it certainly pays off for Sydney. Her team members are loyal, and they give their supervisor the best they have every time.

One time while chatting with Sydney, I complimented her on her listening skills. She said, "Leil, I owe it all to my dad, who was a theatrical lighting designer."

"Your dad?" I asked, surprised.

She continued, "I must have been a typical indifferent teenager because Dad was forever telling me I had to listen better. One time he put his foot down and threatened I'd be grounded unless I played a game he suggested to me. I didn't want that so I grudgingly agreed.

"He told me to imagine I had a big flashlight shining out of my chest. 'Whenever you are talking to someone, turn that flashlight toward the person you're speaking with.'"

"'OK,' I muttered. It felt strange at first. But soon it became a natural habit, and I didn't even have to think about it. I started shining my chest flashlight on everybody I talked to and have done so ever since. I see a big difference in people's reactions to me, and I know I'm not imagining it. So don't thank me, Leil. Thank my dad."

"Aha," I thought, "that's why Sydney appears to be an excellent listener!" For the rest of the time I worked with her, I was conscious of her little trick and noticed how beautifully it worked. It does for me, now, too, and it's become second nature.

LITTLE TRICK #14

The Torso Flashlight

Whenever you're standing talking with someone, do more than turn your head toward the person. Swivel your entire torso like you have a bright flashlight shining out from your chest. Even at a conference table, turn your torso slightly toward the speaker. Everyone you aim your beam toward feels heard, understood, and appreciated, which is crucial to caring communication.

Oh, I should mention a slight gender difference here. If you're a man talking one-on-one with another male, the rules change a bit. If you stand directly face-to-face with each other, it can come across as too personal, perhaps even aggressive. So, gentlemen, when talking to another man, turn ever so slightly to the side. You can also imagine a spotlight coming out of your chest, but make it a wide-angle floodlight that gives you more flexibility and permits you to turn to a slightly less than 45 degree angle. If you're at a desk or conference table, however, you can turn more directly toward another man because the furniture between you serves as your "safety zone."

Because men seldom stand directly face-to-face when talking (unless they're angry), they don't pick up on many of the communication subtleties that females do. So, women, when something breaks down in the communication chain at work, give the guys a break. They're working with a handicap!

14

Don't Give
Hit-and-Run Praise

If a colleague grants you a favor at work or a direct report does a great job on an assignment, of course you thank them. It's only expected, and you'd be rude not to. But what's the real point of saying thank you? It's to express your gratitude and make the recipient feel good about what he's done, right? But the usual "thanks" or even "good job" is as common as fleas on a dog. So when it comes out of your mouth, it's like elevator music. People hardly hear it.

I'd like to share a quick and easy technique that accomplishes the true purpose of a thank you. (And in the process, it makes the recipient want to do *more* for you.) When your supervisor, passing you in the hall, says, "Thanks for finding that document this morning," sure you're pleased. You're happy about her praise, and the pleasure lasts, at least until you get to the end of the hall. But picture this instead. She comes out of her office, makes a trip over to your desk, stops, smiles, looks you straight in the eyes, uses your name, and says, "I am so impressed you were able to find that missing document this morning! Obviously, someone saved it in the wrong folder. But you stayed late yesterday and went through the whole computer until you found the original. You just didn't give up, and I really appreciate it. Thanks so much."

Wow, now you feel fantastic! Your inner smile lingers all day, and while driving home, you're still feeling good about it. At dinner, you might even tell your family what she said. Suddenly you like your supervisor a whole lot more. And naturally, the next time she has a problem, you'll definitely go the extra mile for her. It's a win-win situation for both of you, all because she gave you a few more sentences of gratitude.

Now let's say a colleague you were never really crazy about, Kaylee, asks you to proofread a report she wrote. "Geeze, she never did anything for me," you grouse. "Why should I help her out? Besides I've got enough work of my own. I don't have time for this." But being the accommodating person that you are, you say, "Sure, Kaylee, leave it right here."

At the end of the afternoon, you take it to her desk with the markings you made. She glances at it, and of course you expect a thank you. But instead, she looks up at you with a grateful smile and says, "Oh my gosh. That's wonderful! You did a lot of work on it. I felt so guilty asking you, but I was at my wit's end. I knew I could turn to you, and I'm so appreciative. Your writing is so much more professional than mine and . . ."

Now you're thinking, "Hey, this woman's not so bad after all!" In fact, suddenly you have warm feelings toward Kaylee and the seeds of a professional friendship are planted, just because she spent a few extra seconds expressing her gratitude.

Whenever a colleague or report does something well or grants you a favor, keep your praise going. Stretch it out a bit. Give more details. Tell the person how it affected you and *why* you're grateful.

One last example: Suppose you traded a day off with a coworker at your request. When it comes time to say thanks, amplify your words of gratitude by giving her specifics on what the favor did for you. Something like, "Your trading with me was super because I was way behind in my holiday shopping. I don't know what I would have done without that extra day. My son would've been devastated without his train set, and he should thank you, too! I really appreciate it. I hope I can do something nice for you sometime." Now that gives your compliment some oomph!

 LITTLE TRICK #15

Prolong Your Praise

S-t-r-e-t-c-h out your compliment. A simple sentence isn't enough when a coworker or a report does something you're grateful for. Go for three sentences minimum! The melody of your protracted praise is sweet music to their ears. Like making love, the longer it lasts, the better it is!

Special note to supervisors: Please don't let this one slip through the cracks. When praising someone, don't just keep walking. Stop, pause, look directly in your employee's eyes, and only then deliver your kudos. Prolonged praise is extremely potent when coming from you. It wins their respect, loyalty, and their desire to please you.

How to Make Your Kudos *Extra* Special

No matter what industry you're in or what position you hold—from cleaning person in a grimy factory to vice president of a multinational conglomerate—every employee has a boss. And all workers want to impress theirs. Competition for the boss's favor is universal, so here's a quick tip to show you're a caring, sharing individual, which, unfortunately, is becoming an endangered species in certain cutthroat companies. This little trick makes your praise extra special and enhances your on-the-job relationships.

★ LITTLE TRICK #16

Make Your Compliment Count

Give your praise extra punch by choosing a moment when you and the coworker are casually chatting with your boss. Then find a smooth way to tell your superior about the fantastic job your coworker did. Your well-timed kudos will thrill your colleague and make you look good in your boss's eyes, too.

Here's an e-mail tip that, incidentally, also makes you look good. When writing your boss on a certain matter, if appropriate, praise a colleague's contribution.

15

"Good Eye Contact" Is Not Enough!

One of the simplest and most obvious ways to demonstrate you are a caring individual is to give everyone you work with a gift. Not a physical one. Not something you pay money for. But a precious offering to make each colleague feel special. And it's free! The gift is "locking eyes" with everyone you're talking to.

We often withhold eye contact from people who bore us or rub us the wrong way. Lack of eye contact can signal antipathy, aversion, animosity, or fear. People often shield their eyes or look away from terrifying scenes in a movie, but we instinctively look into the eyes of those we respect, admire, and appreciate. I'm sure you've seen proud parents looking lovingly at their infants for long periods of time, and lovers gazing into each other's eyes seemingly forever. Warm eye contact is a sign of approval and appreciation, respect and reverence.

When your eyes lock with a coworker's, intense uncon-scious forces take over. A study called "An Eye Movement Phenomenon Relating to Attention, Thought and Anxiety" published in *Perceptual and Motor Skills* proved that, dur-ing extended contact, an adrenaline-like substance courses through people's veins and increases their heartbeat. Concentrated eye contact is a near magical state of two brains simultaneously scanning each other, processing what they're hearing, and deciding how they feel about each other and what's being said. No other communication method matches it—not phoning, not videoconferencing, and def-initely nothing digital.

Eye contact has even more implications on the job, because many more factors come into it. Are you in com-petition with the person? Has he always been straight with you? Has she ever been petty? And who wants what from whom? Additionally, whatever happens during this particu-lar encounter shapes the timbre of the next. When you tap this powerful tool, you can even guide your coworkers to a certain extent. Leonard Bernstein was known to conduct an entire orchestra with just his eyes and eyebrows. You may have had a boss or two who controlled meetings that way. When he looked your way, you knew it was your turn to speak. When she rolled her eyes, you closed your mouth. If he nodded approvingly, you kept talking. When she squinted, you felt obligated to explain yourself.

It's an unfortunate fact of life that sometimes you have to camouflage your real feelings at work. You must calibrate what is strategic to reveal and what is not, then train your eyes to express precisely the message you wish to transmit. Don't forget that at work you're playing by different rules. No matter how much you disagree or are bored by what someone is saying, you must avoid looking disinterested or disdainful. Successfully concealing that shows you have good leadership qualities and keeps workers connected to you. When you master the art of superior eye contact, you'll be handsomely rewarded in the currency of everyone's support and respect.

In the cutting-edge field called neurorobotics, which combines neuroscience and artificial intelligence, roboticists don't overlook the emotional significance of eye contact. They invest millions trying to make their humanoids have just the right amount with you. They haven't yet succeeded, and just think, you can do it for free! Let your imagination help you with the following technique to show that you're interested in what your boss and colleagues have to say, enjoy listening to them, and are anxious to hear more. It involves the speed with which you break eye contact and return to it.

★ LITTLE TRICK #17

Lock Eyes

Whenever talking with coworkers, envision a rubber band stretching between your eyeballs and theirs. When you must occasionally look away, tug your eyes away slowly, reluctantly, as if you're having difficulty stretching the rubber band. Don't forget to look thoughtful and attentive during those occasional moments. Then quickly click your eyes back to *lock position* with theirs as though you're eagerly awaiting their next words.

Not only does this powerful little trick gain allies at work, it wins over enemies. And there's yet another big benefit. When you keep your eyes on theirs even during the silences, you come across as being an insightful abstract thinker who integrates incoming data more easily than concrete thinkers. Individuals more focused on ideas, rather than their own subjective views or feelings about the relationship, aren't as disturbed by intense eye contact because their minds are busy absorbing the concepts.

When Talking with Several Colleagues

Do the following during a meeting or when conversing with a small group to give you the look of a leader interested in all sides of the situation being discussed.

Watch the Listeners

Occasionally take your eyes off the person who is speaking and watch one or more of the other listeners. This gives the impression you have a thorough understanding of the situation and are searching for more subtleties to round out your knowledge. It also makes you look like an evaluator judging other employees' comprehension and reactions. *A note of caution:* Don't overdo it or it could look creepy! An additional benefit is that it makes the person you're watching feel that you care about how it affects her, too.

Seeing Eye to Eye in Today's Global Economy

I would be remiss if I didn't mention one last point. No doubt you're aware of the cultural differences in the meaning of eye contact. In certain Asian countries, direct eye contact does not represent honesty, confidence, interest, and forthrightness as it does in the West. There, strong eye contact can be viewed as rude or disrespectful. I knew this consciously, but once when giving a seminar in Singapore, it staggered me. Apparently, just because I was the presenter, my students had dubbed me a "figure of authority." Therefore, in one-on-one conversations, they hesitated to look into my eyes. If I hadn't known about this cultural difference, I would have thought they disliked me or were totally disinterested in my words.

Please understand that if some of your Asian coworkers give you less eye contact, it doesn't mean they don't respect you. In fact, it could just be the opposite! The same is true with Native Americans, and it gets even more complicated than that. The French give much more eye contact, even to strangers on the street. And in Muslim countries, beware of making eye contact with the other sex.

Bottom line: Big players on the international scene scoop up every speck of information they can find on cultural diversity before meeting with people from a different culture. Never forget that one of the most powerful communication skills in your arsenal is staring right back at you every time you look into a mirror.

Now let's talk about some more spoken ways to show you care.

16

How to Establish Rapport Without Sacrificing Your Principles

A human resources professional taught me this little trick that works wonders in everyday relationships with coworkers and makes even the tough ones more bearable. It saves you hours of having to listen to gripers, gossips, yellers, and a variety of other unsavory workplace types.

I first witnessed its efficacy at a company that hired me to help pull it out of the communication quicksand it was drowning in. Savannah, the HR director, had accomplished the delicate task of being liked and respected by everyone she worked with. Her office was a revolving door of employees anxious to share their highly emotional situations. Because they thoroughly trusted her confidentiality, she invited me, with the employees' permission of course, to sit in on some of her sessions. I heard a wide variety of grumbling such as . . .

> "My boss looks over my shoulder every second. I think 'micromanager' is her middle name."

> "I am way underpaid for my position."

> "He shovels too much work my way and keeps piling it on."

And of course they griped about their colleagues who are sloppy, rude, whiners, gossips, pranksters, nonstop talkers, human loudspeakers, and untold others. One employee even said she wanted to push a certain colleague down the elevator shaft. It was scary stuff.

After sitting in on several of Savannah's sessions and seeing the peevish employees walk out much calmer, I complimented her skill, saying, "You are absolutely amazing. The company is so fortunate to have you." Then I ventured, "So what's the secret of your success dealing with all their diverse problems?"

Thanking me for the compliment, she replied, "Well, there is one thing I do a lot. It's really simple. While an employee is describing a problem to me, I listen with my eyes as much as my ears and try to see how they *feel* about whatever they're saying. I need to determine their emotions and pick up on any undercurrents."

"For example?" I asked.

"Well, most of them are angry at their bosses or are exasperated about a company policy or customer. Tons of them tell me about a particular colleague who is driving them berserk. No matter what they're upset about, I don't say anything at first. I just listen, and watch. Then, when I figure out how they're feeling, I comment, but just on their emotion."

I found her technique fascinating, and it worked like a charm. I started calling it "Savannah's secret formula," and was on the lookout for it at every session she let me attend. Sure enough, after listening to various distraught employees talk it out, she would say things like . . .

"I know how *troubling* that must be."

"That must be so *aggravating*."

"I understand why you are *so upset*."

"Yes, that is *disappointing*."

Savannah continued putting the employees' emotions in sympathetic words. Only then would this top professional communicator start using some of the more traditional HR professionals' methods. You certainly don't need to be in HR to benefit from this technique. You'd be surprised at how it helps with your office relationships, and it's so easy to do!

State Their Sentiments

Most people who are upset go on and on just to get you to understand their agitation. Don't overdo your sympathetic response (as I've heard some people do, and it can be irritating), but by occasionally stating their sentiment from what you observe, you're *already* giving them what they were after: Your understanding. Your sympathy. When you occasionally comment on a colleague's emotions, you create a bond and can make a quicker escape. It also frees you up from having to offer an opinion on the situation, which could open a can of worms for you.

17

Is It Better to Be Liked or Respected at Work?

sometimes ask my consulting clients this question during casual conversations. Quite a few say, "Being respected is most important." Don't they realize there's a glass ceiling above the heads of those who feel that way? It's not one of gender or race. This one is molded from the hidden hostility of their colleagues. Those upward strivers are struggling to crawl up a slippery slope, because without some of the caring ways of dealing with colleagues, they have enemies salivating to see them fall. Others say, "Being liked is more important." But that sometimes means giving in to people and sacrificing your principles. A strong leader doesn't do that. I promise you, though, there are ways to garner both respect *and* warmth from everyone you work with.

How to Be Both

When the "liked or respected" question comes up in my seminars, I occasionally ask the students, "Have you ever been disciplined by a boss you respected *and* liked—and still do?" Only a few hands go up. I then ask if anyone would be comfortable sharing his or her story. I especially admired a young woman named Shauna in one of my classes who volunteered. I was impressed because it was at an in-house seminar for employees who work at the same company, which makes it doubly tough to share personal information.

Shauna was a salesperson at a promotional giveaways company and started by telling us about a boss she had last year who made life for her a living hell. "Part of my job was to gather ideas about product improvement every month from the whole team and write up the suggestions for my boss," she said. "I liked this assignment because I'd always prided myself on being a pretty good writer. In fact, I majored in English at college and was hoping to get published someday.

"But I began to doubt my writing ability when my boss gave me negative feedback on my first report. He called me into his office, scowled, and shoved the last report across the desk under my nose. He'd scribbled all over it with a red marker. He'd also written disparaging comments in the margins like 'Too flowery,' 'Ick,' 'Bad writing,' and 'Weasel words.' I was crushed and felt I no longer had writing talent. I asked him what I should do next. He growled, 'If I were you, I'd do the whole thing over again.'"

Then suddenly Shauna's face broke into a big smile. "He was only there for a few more months before he got fired." The class cheered because apparently everyone knew who she'd been talking about and felt the same way.

I found her story interesting but was confused because my question had been about having a boss who disciplined you whom you still had warm feelings for. "And after the way he handled that, you still like and respect him?" I asked.

"Oh no," she laughed, "that was my *next* supervisor. And still is. Her name is Daphne." The other participants smiled and nodded hearing her name. Shauna continued, "Well, after giving her my next monthly report on the findings, Daphne called me into her office. Needless to say, I was pretty nervous due to my last experience. But the first thing she said was, 'Shauna, that report was beautifully written. You really have a knack for writing!'"

"I wanted to hug her!" she exclaimed. "Hearing my new supervisor say that was super. Then Daphne explained to me that, unfortunately, the production department usually works from flat descriptions with bullet points. She called me over to her side of the desk so we could sit side by side and look at my report together. She took the time to make sure I understood precisely what she was saying about each item, and then we shaved them down and listed them by bullet points.

"At the end of the meeting, Daphne told me that she hated to see my talent going to waste on writing boring text. 'But that's the form we must give it to them in,' she shrugged. I agreed.

"Anyway, Daphne's great, and I'm really pleased I could get her what she wanted. I worked extra hard at it after that, and she really appreciates it and often tells me so."

I smiled to myself because I knew precisely what Daphne had accomplished and how she did it. She had corrected her employee without stomping on her ego by using a technique I heard about a long time ago. I don't know whom to give credit to, but thank you whoever you are, because I've used it ever since. It's called the "hamburger technique."

The Never-Fail Technique

The following is the best way I've yet found for giving constructive criticism or feedback, and the beauty of it is that it's not just for bosses. It works wonders when trying to cure an annoying colleague of aggravating habits. Here's how it works.

Imagine a big juicy hamburger. On the top there's half of a nice soft squishy bun. Under that, there's the meat, the substance of the burger. There might even be a few frills like lettuce, tomatoes, and onions. But the reason you bought the burger was for the beef. At the bottom of the burger, there's the other half of the soft bun. (For those of you who are vegetarians, you can think of it as first "the good stuff," then "the bad stuff," and then "the good stuff" again.)

In Shauna's case, the top bun was her supervisor complimenting her writing. Under that was "the meat," how to do the report correctly. Daphne then ended the session with another nice soft bun.

The Hamburger Technique

Whenever you must criticize people you work with, the first step is to give praise about something specific involving what you must correct them on. Step two: Give 'em the meat, the behavior you want them to change. Step three: End the session with more praise.

If the individual you are trying to correct needs serious schmoozing, decorate your compliment with some other welcome words. Think of those as the ketchup, mustard, cheese, and onions. If you have more than one grievance, separate the two harsh "meat" parts with another soft bun. That's a Big Whopper!

You Don't Have to Be the Boss to Use This Little Trick

This technique also works beautifully for stamping out colleagues' annoying habits. Let me tell you how I first used it more than 20 years ago. At one company I consulted for, the only extra computer was in an empty cubicle, which I used.

The woman sitting in the cubicle next to me was an incontinent hummer and would sometimes croon songs to herself as she was working. It drove me nuts, and at one point, I thought, "Enough is enough. I have to deal with this." My crooning cubicle neighbor was really full of herself, and I knew she wouldn't respond well. As I was racking my brain on how to deal with this irritating woman, I remembered I'd once read about the hamburger technique.

The next time I saw her in the lunchroom, I told her what a beautiful singing voice she had. This thrilled her, and she exuberated that she'd been taking singing lessons. We chatted about that for a while, and only then did I mention that sometimes I overheard her singing to herself. I apologized and said, "It sounds so nice that I can't ignore it, and sometimes I can't concentrate on my work." We laughed about how her songs might have the same powerful effect on her fans one day, and I asked if she'd ever posted her songs on YouTube.

It worked! I never heard another song coming through the cubicle wall. This woman got the point, and it caused no hard feelings. I've used the hamburger technique ever since in hundreds of different situations. Try it the next time that something really irritates you. You'll see what I mean.

18

E-mail Amity

If you've used the Internet, then you likely have an e-mail address. And if you have an e-mail address, then you've written and read e-mail. Chapter over. You've mastered communicating by e-mail, right? You wrote what you wanted and got your point across. Right? No one was hurt by or took offense your e-mail? No one misunderstood your e-mail or IM? No one read too deep into your message and found hidden meanings you never intended, right?

Of course recipients screwed up your intent! They read your message, processed it, and their brain turned it into whatever *they* wanted it to be. From the first line to your signature, how long it took you to answer, who you cc'd and who you didn't, your words are forever stamped in stone as proof of whatever they want to accuse you of. (Deleting it on your computers or other devices doesn't work because a good IT department can retrieve texts or messages that were deleted months or even years ago.) You can't win. Or can you?

Well, yes. Because there are ways to keep your e-mails from lighting a spark that can turn into a company explosion. I won't get into too many particular tips because there are excellent ones plastered all over the web such as . . .

- Optimize for mobile.

- Avoid attachments unless expected.

- Use short relevant subject lines (less than 35 characters).

- Don't change subject lines mid-thread.

- Write short paragraphs and keep your e-mail as brief as possible.

- Bullet points are good.

- All caps is shouting.

- All lowercase is childish.

- Never assume privacy.

- Watch out for Reply All if you didn't intend to.

- Be sensitive to time zones.

- Run spell-check and proofread.

- Avoid weekend or after-hours business messages.

- Be judicious with BCC, because it can make you look sneaky.

- Make sure all links work.

- So your message doesn't get lost in the hundreds that the recipients may be faced with when they come to work, don't send until shortly *after* their usual arrival time.

Sweet Sign-Offs and Signatures

This late in the game, however, I've found some people still get screwy with their signatures, so let's address that for a moment. If you're writing outside your company, a simple automatically generated footer with just your company information suffices. (You don't even need that if you're writing to someone with whom you work continually or closely.) You can precede the footer with a simple "Many thanks," "Appreciated," or "Cheers." Avoid signatures with flamboyant fonts, photos, flashing company logos, or pretentious graphics that take ages to download. (Too bad there isn't an "unsubscribe" button for some people you have to deal with!)

Here's a little trick, a thoroughly professional way to give your messages warmth, that I haven't come across anywhere else. When writing to a customer, colleague, or boss, most employees use the recipient's name right off the bat. Something like, "Hi Hayden," "Hello Hayden," "Hey Hayden," or maybe just plain "Hayden," But don't let this attention-getter, the person's name, lose punch by putting it in its expected place. Make it work for you by saving it for *another* part of your message either to flag an important point or strengthen a bond at the end of your message.

Just like people perk up when hearing their name in a crowd, they'll pay more attention when their name jumps out at them later in your message. Let's say you need Hayden's response to a question by a certain time. If you just write, "I need your answer by 2 p.m. on Friday," he might miss it. Flag the significance by slapping his name smack-dab next to it. Write, "I need your answer, Hayden, by 2 p.m.," and he will pay more attention to the 2 p.m. deadline.

Also using the recipient's name as the final word of your message adds a caring touch. You've probably heard that people's names are "the sweetest sound in the English language" to them. So instead of opening your message with it as expected, close your e-mail with "It was good working with you, Hayden." Or "I'm looking forward to hearing from you, Hayden."

★ LITTLE TRICK #21

Punch Up Your Points with Their Name

Use the recipient's name to your advantage in your e-mail messages. If you want a particular point to stand out in the middle of your message, flag it by putting the person's name right next to it. And you can make all your office messages sound more personal and caring by using people's names as the last word of your e-mail. Just don't overdo it. Writing the recipient's name once or twice in your message is enough.

Make Your Messages Exciting
(Without Emojis)

Almost everyone secretly enjoys smiley faces with devil horns, hearts, monkeys, surprise and shrug emojis. How did we ever express ourselves without silly little pictures to show how we feel? Today, when using emojis, the problem isn't so much a generational gap as a professionalism gap. Times are changing fast, but many still feel an emoji is proof that the writer has a weak vocabulary. So what's an emoji-addicted professional to do?

Here are some tips: Don't send an emoji to people who are above you in the hierarchy unless they send one to you first. Avoid them in work communications to people at other companies, even if they're good friends. If your e-mail is shared, you and your company can quickly lose credibility. (A note on personal communication: Don't send emojis to anyone born before 1980 unless you know them well.) Then there's the ultimate emoji, the GIF. It's an emoji on steroids. So much can go wrong sending those in a professional context that you should forget they even exist.

What about the original emoji, the exclamation point? Now that people are drowning in emojis, their senses have dulled, and many are decorating their messages with too many exclamation points. If you have more than one or two in a message, recipients will suspect that you don't know how to use the English language to express your sentiments. Limit the number and use your computer's thesaurus feature instead. People with rich vocabularies are considered more creative, educated, and intelligent. And to think, all you need to do is click on a word. Dozens of choices pop up to enhance your messages without emojis or exclamation points.

19

Can You Be Too Nice at Work?

Some employees go overboard with wanting to be liked, so they needlessly suffer in silence and don't speak up when they should. For example, I've heard hundreds of complaints like these about office conditions, and many of them are warranted.

"There's never any toilet paper in the john."

"It's as cold as a crypt in here."

"The noise from the air conditioner's driving me crazy."

"The chairs are as hard as rocks."

The first step is to ask yourself, "Is this something I can put up with? Can I just chew it up, spit it out, and get on with my day?" If so, give that a shot first, because nobody respects a whiner. But if you don't speak up about an intolerable condition at work, you might find yourself in the same situation as Polly, the parrot.

Oh, you haven't heard about Polly, the parrot, who spoke 14 languages? Let me tell you about this rare bird. A loving husband was searching for an anniversary gift for his dear wife of 20 years. As he ambled by a pet store, a parrot squawked out to him, "Hello there. I speak 14 languages."

"What?" the astonished man said, coming to a screeching halt and spinning around.

"*Oui*," the parrot said in French.

"Are . . . Are . . . Are you serious?" the man asked

"*Certo*," the parrot replied in Italian.

"No!" the man exclaimed.

"*Sí*," the parrot countered in Spanish.

The man raced into the pet store and asked the owner how much the rare bird cost. "Five thousand dollars, sir."

"Five thousand dollars!" the man shrieked.

"Well, yes, sir," the owner replied, "because she's the only parrot in the world who speaks 14 languages."

"Well," the man thought to himself, "my wife is a language buff, and this is our twentieth anniversary."

"All right," he said with a sigh, writing out a big fat check. He packed Polly (Polly Lingual was her full name) under his arm and headed home with the prize parrot. He decided to mount Polly's new perch right over the kitchen sink, where his wife would be sure to see the talented rare bird when she returned from shopping. As he was placing Polly up on her new perch, he suddenly slapped his head realizing he had forgotten the birdseed! He raced back to the store.

When he got back home, his wife had already returned from her shopping, and she greeted him at the door. She threw her arms around him and exclaimed, "I didn't think you'd even remember our anniversary, let alone surprise me with such a wonderful gift!" The man beamed. She continued, "Darling, you remembered how much I love pheasant."

"Pheasant?" he gasped.

"Yes," she replied. "I've got him plucked. I've got him slit. I've got him stuffed. He's already in the oven, and he'll be ready to eat in about half an hour."

"You've got him what? You've got him where? That was no pheasant," he howled. "That was a parrot, and what's more, that parrot cost five thousand dollars because it spoke 14 languages!"

"Oh really," replied his wife. "Well then, why didn't he speak up?"

You've probably guessed the message in this fable: If you don't speak up . . . well, I won't say your goose will be cooked like poor Polly's. But if you don't tell a relevant person about the problem, the first thought will be, "Schnook, well, why didn't you *say* something?" Without mincing words, I call this technique . . .

LITTLE TRICK #22

Put Up, Shut Up, or Speak Up

The next time you're tempted to complain, stop and think about it. Is there anything you could possibly do to alleviate the situation? If so, do it now. And if your hands are tied, mention the problem to your boss—not as a complaint but as an FYI. Be sure to have some suggested resolutions to present at the same time.

20

Should You Have Close Friends at Work?

Wow, that's the million-dollar question. For happiness and fulfillment in life, we all need friends. Friends on the job make the workday much more pleasant. In fact, friends (the flesh-and-blood ones you've actually met and often see, not the social media ones) are one of the greatest joys in life. But what's your definition of a real friend? Most people feel it's someone you can share your innermost thoughts and dreams with. It's someone who is there for you no matter what. It's someone who has your best interests at heart.

Now think of the people you work with. Do you think it's safe to share your innermost thoughts and dreams with them? Do you think many of them would be there for you no matter what? If push came to shove, do you really think they'd have *your* best interest at heart? Or their own?

Sometimes it's difficult to know whom you can trust. In my seminars I've heard scads of stories about coworkers who pretend to be chums but would throw you under the bus in a heartbeat. One of my students, Pasha, told me that at her first job she became fast friends with a woman who'd helped with some of her work. "When we became very close," she said, "I started sharing some of my personal problems. I even confided that I'd once had a drinking problem and told her Alcoholics Anonymous meetings were a godsend because they'd helped me quit."

Pasha continued, "The following week, five or six of us were talking on our lunch hour, and one of the guys in the group asked me, 'Hey, have you been keeping up with your AA meetings?' I wanted to die because my supervisor was there and knew nothing about them! My so-called friend probably told everybody."

Times are rapidly changing, and my advice 10 years ago would have been, "Try to keep your social and work life separate." But in today's progressive companies, that's inconceivable, and often by design. To draw the best talent from millennials, gen Xers, and gen Yers, smart organizations—in addition to having a fantastic digital infrastructure—are creating workspaces that encourage collaboration and the ability to balance work and leisurely activities. Forward-thinking companies recognize that friendships are a basic need. Laugh, play, collaborate—enjoy your colleagues—but heed the warning label on giving coworkers too much information about your personal life.

If your ranks differ, close office friendships have a little skull and crossbones label. Several months ago, one of my students, Serena, who supervised an all-female marketing department at a cosmetics firm, asked if she could talk to me for a few minutes after class. She said she had a question. "Of course, Serena, ask away. I hope I have an answer."

"Well, Leil, headquarters gave me the go-ahead to promote one of my direct reports to team leader. I'd like to choose Lynn, who stands head and shoulders above the rest. She's super creative, always gets her reports in on time, and has excellent follow-through. But I can't decide whether to give the promotion."

"Why not?" I asked. "Well," she continued, "during our breaks, I talk with Lynn a lot, and we often sit together in the company lunchroom. We became friends out of the office too."

"Oops," I thought, "here comes a familiar problem."

"Well, now Lynn and I have lunch together several times a month at Applebee's. Last week I felt some women across the restaurant staring at us. When I looked over, I saw that three of them reported to me. As soon as I looked up, they made nosedives back into their sandwiches pretending they hadn't seen us. Now I hesitate to promote Lynn because everyone would think I was playing favorites."

I told Serena I understood, but not knowing all the subtleties and nuances of her other relationships at work, I hesitated to advise her.

However, I want to share her story with you so you can think twice if you're ever in a situation where it might look like friendship with a coworker is clouding your judgment. We all need friends, and the workplace is changing drastically as you're reading this. Experts speak of the "social workforce," in which the people you work with will become, in a sense, "family." This is lovely, but getting too close to someone on the job is dangerous, especially if your positions differ. While enjoying your office relationships, tread carefully to avoid cliques, gossip, and jealousy, and don't give your workplace pal TMI (too much information) about yourself—meaning anything you wouldn't be comfortable with the whole company knowing.

★ LITTLE TRICK #23

Take Care What You Share at Work

As corporate communication becomes more virtual, flesh-and-blood relationships become all the more precious, but be careful when it comes to confidentiality. Don't share secrets or talk about what you feel are your weaknesses. I've heard hundreds of sad stories about the problems this has caused. Backstabbing and slander are just the tip of the iceberg. Bonding is beautiful—but beware!

To express that you are a truly caring person at work, use all the techniques we've discussed. Treat your colleagues' egos like eggshells, make your smile mean something, state their sentiments for connection, amplify their earned praise, put professional warmth in your e-mails, turn fully toward the person you're talking with, and, of course, use your most powerful communication tool, your eyes. Connect with coworkers in these ways, but don't make the mistake of getting *too* close and letting your guard down. It's not called the "corporate jungle" for nothing!

21

A Primal Need

Before I tell you my view on this volatile subject, I want to share my deeply felt sentiment about physical human touch. It could be a brief pat on the back, a friendly hair ruffling, a guy-type shoulder punch, girls' amicable arm linking, an exuberant high five, or even an innocent touch of one woman's hand on another female employee's. Touch is a powerful and poignant force in our lives. Your need for it began when you were enveloped in the close quarters of your mother's womb for nine months. And it doesn't stop at birth. The moment you made your screaming, flailing entrance into the world, you continually needed touch for healthy development. Something as simple as a loving touch has been proved to make the difference between life and death for children in an orphanage, and its potency remains throughout life until the very end. Nursing homes report the phenomenal effect of human touch on residents' health, happiness, and longevity.

I care intensely about this, so before I put my case to rest, let me share a bit more. Studies show that the brief compassionate touch of a doctor makes patients think the physician stayed twice as long. And students receiving a supportive pat on the back or touch on the arm were far more likely to volunteer for projects. Dentists whose hands brushed their patients' faces while working on them got more referrals. In yet another study, nurses had to warn women entering a brain scanner that they would receive a shock. The MRI showed that the women's fear circuits relaxed when the nurses lightly touched them. I have probably gone on too long here, but the point is paramount. Touch is powerful. Touch is crucial. Touch is a primal need. But in the workplace, touch is a definite no! It's clear and simple: no touching at work.

In the 1990s during the war on drugs, the big advertising slogan was "Just Say No." These words were a powerful deterrent and now, especially since the long overdue war on sexual harassment, we must resist any form of physical contact at work, no matter how innocent. Women, we must curb our natural instinct to put our arms around a dear friend at work to comfort her. Men, you should even swear off buddy-style back pats and arm punches. And when it comes to any kind of touch with the opposite sex, no matter how innocent, *just say no!*

"Do Not Touch"

Touch with your eyes, touch with your smile, and touch with your warm words. But don't touch with your bodies. Imagine everyone you work with is wearing a "Do Not Touch" label. Other than a friendly handshake on the job, save the warm friendship signals for friends who don't work at your company. Hands off at work. Period.

Now let's move on to the next crucial element for career success: communicating your ideas clearly and understanding what your coworkers are saying.

PART III

CLARITY

22

How to "See"
What They're Saying

So what is clear communicating at work? Sounds simple enough. It's telling coworkers or your boss something, and they understand. Then they tell you something, and you understand. No problem, right?

Whoa! Then why are there so many communication problems at work? Because communication is a two-way street, and you are responsible for *both* sides: you as the speaker and you as the listener. You'll find hundreds of books on better communication, but not one on listening comes to mind. I mean, would you have shelled out your hard-earned cash if this one was titled, *How to Listen to Anyone at Work*? Not likely, because listening doesn't sound like much fun. Don't worry, though. I won't take much of your time on this boring subject other than to restate how critical, consequential, conclusive, crucial, major, meaningful, and momentous it is—and central to your success at work. So let's get listening out of the way before we get to the more fun part, talking.

On average, the human mind races four to six times faster than any speaker's words. So unless you're hearing something that impacts your life in an important way, your mind wanders. Plus, to respond appropriately or act on what someone has said, you must not only listen but actually remember it! Therein lies the problem. According to the widely accepted "Cone of Experience" researched by Edgar Dale, we unfortunately only remember 20 percent of what we hear. But here's the good news and the basis of this little trick. Human beings remember more than half of what they both hear *and* see. That's why it's easier to recall details in a movie you've seen rather than a story you've heard. In a film, images, movements, and colors back up the sounds. So the trick is to turn the speaker's words into something you "see" too. Make it an audio*visual* experience by listening with your eyes too.

While your boss, colleague, customer, or report is talking to you, imagine two miniature screens floating in front of your eyes—sort of like wearing those clunky augmented reality glasses. While listening, create pictures or visualize what the speaker is saying. Bring her words to life in your mind's eye like a movie. Now you have no time to be bored, because you're not slowing your thought processes down; you're speeding them up! You are flushing out her flat words into clear 3-D pictures for yourself, which makes listening much more exciting—and memorable.

LITTLE TRICK #25

Be an Audiovisual Listener

Don't just listen with your ears; listen with your eyes as well. Turn them into imaginary cameras to create a theatrical production of what you are both hearing and seeing. Not only do you "get the picture" more clearly; you also remember it longer. And it's fun, because your imagination is working overtime.

23

Make Their Words
Your Words

It's human instinct. Whenever colleagues are talking, we tend to interject our own thoughts and form opinions every step of the way. You can't help it. You're smart, and since your mind works much faster than they can speak, naturally you make judgments. But this is dangerous, because you can come to incorrect conclusions before the speaker even finishes. Sure, I could tell you, "Reserve your judgments for later," but you know that's impossible. Unfortunately, forming premature opinions is dropping an enormous roadblock in the two-way street called "Clear Communicating." Here's a technique to prevent you from that common communication-killer and, at the same time, clarify your understanding of what's being said.

For this little trick you put on a different hat. Now you're no longer a filmmaker; you are a simultaneous translator. Translating from another language is a tough challenge, but it's a snap when it's English to English. Translators at the United Nations interpreting Spanish to Serbian, or Slovenian to Swahili, or Hungarian to Hindi, don't have time to form opinions on what they're hearing. They simply repeat the speaker's words in a different language. So try this: As you're listening to someone talk, repeat silently what the speaker is saying, but put it in simpler terms—yours! Translate, sentence by sentence, what you're hearing into your own words.

Suppose you have a self-important manufacturing client who is expounding, in his own pompous business jargon, "The name of the game for us is maximization." In your mind, translate that into your words, "He wants to balance price and output for more profit."

He continues, "Differentiation is of paramount importance." You silently say, "He wants to show off the benefits of what he makes compared with the benefits of competing products."

He then states, "That's where electronic customer profiling helps." You again, "My client wants to collect extensive information on his existing customers."

"We must integrate client-driven data into our strategy." To keep your mind from wandering, silently say, "Our plans must take into account what the customer wants."

Your sentences are a lot clearer and a heck of a lot easier for you to remember because *you* said them. You are simply repeating what the client was saying, but putting it into your own words. This technique also works wonders for your memory, because we recall most of what we ourselves say, but only a tiny percentage of what our colleagues and customers utter.

Be a Simultaneous Translator

Silently paraphrase what the speaker is saying in your own words, because you'll understand more clearly and remember it longer. You'll also be less apt to interrupt or form premature judgments. And, hey, this one is fun, too. It even keeps you awake while listening to blowhards!

24

It's a "Communication Problem"! Duh

When on-the-job problems come up, workers around the world shrug their shoulders, grind their teeth, or throw up their hands in exasperation sputtering . . .

> *"Es un problema de comunicación."*

> *"C'est un problème de communication."*

> *"Es ist ein problem mit communikation."*

> "It's a communication problem!"

If international negotiations break down or a problem arises when employees work with colleagues in other countries, people often blame it on a language barrier. Yes, that contributes, but it's seldom the root of the problem. Good communication starts with stating something clearly and making sure it's understood.

When you need to tell coworkers something in person, you talk to them, right? And when that's done, most people figure they've communicated their thoughts. Not so fast! Telling is not a one-way street. Let's say you must convey a concept to three coworkers in the next 10 minutes. First you say to one colleague, "Let me know if the customer received the product today." Second, you ask your boss to give you information on a client by the end of the day. Third, you tell your direct report to bring you the figures from the last quarter.

Five o'clock rolls around, and you still have no idea if the client received the product. As well, your boss hasn't yet given you the information you need, and there's no sign of the figures from the last quarter on your desk. But wait a minute—you told each of them in plain English precisely what you wanted. Are they being uncooperative, hostile, or what? Didn't they believe you needed that information today? Maybe you throw up your hands and conclude they're just dense. Only one thing is clear. Communication obviously failed somewhere between *your* transmission and *their* reception.

I'm sure it's happened the other way around, too. How many times has a frustrated boss grumbled, "I told you to do that yesterday!" But you know she didn't. Or an exasperated colleague accuses, "You weren't listening to me." You'd feel rude contradicting, but you know you always listen well.

There's a reason stores give customers receipts. It's to clear up any misunderstandings about what the buyer bought. Let's say you purchase several items at the grocery store. You stroll home looking forward to sinking your teeth into one of the Twinkies you just bought. You open the bag, but no Twinkies! You decide to race back to the store to demand your Twinkies, and on the way out, you glance at the grocery receipt. It's not listed! Oops, you forgot to buy the Twinkies. Open and shut case, it's your fault. The receipt is the proof.

If a problem arises at work after you've explained something to a colleague or report, who is at fault isn't as clear and can cause huge problems. For something simple you'd feel insolent asking, "Did you understand what I just said?" However, if you want to be sure anything is clear, you *must* get a receipt. A paper one isn't necessary of course, but you should consciously wait for either a silent or spoken acknowledgment that the person "got it." Consummate communicators confirm not only that they put their ideas across clearly, but that their message was received with comprehension.

You must make completely certain your listeners understand what you're saying every step of the way. Just slapping your words on their plate like a frozen steak doesn't mean they'll recognize that it's meat they must thaw, cook, and eat. Wait to see the lump in their throat as they swallow it. Or in this case, a clear visual sign of comprehension in whatever form it takes. Waiting for it is well worth the time it takes to avoid later mistrust, anger, or the accusatory, "You never said that." If you don't see that signal, keep talking until you're sure they "got it."

Wait for Their "I Got It" Receipt

Silent receipts come in many forms—a slight nod, a smile, or even an expression of understanding in the listener's eyes. If you get a quizzical look, a head tilt, an eye squint, a bemused frown, or the all-too-common blank stare, don't stop there. Explain further. Keep talking until you are 100 percent sure your listeners grasped exactly what you were saying. Keep your eyes on the listeners the entire time until you see that they "got it."

25

Put Some Life in Your Listening

An association of hearing-impaired individuals booked me for a presentation and told me the audience would have various hearing challenges, ranging from partially hearing-impaired to completely deaf. They invited me to a briefing to learn about the group's special needs. Naturally, I was asked to speak more slowly during my talk, raise the volume on my microphone, use larger gestures, and never turn my face away from the audience. I had assumed these things, but I inadvertently learned something extraordinary from the group, a technique that has helped me in subsequent communications with everyone.

Because these folks were hard of hearing, they gave me a slight nod during the meeting, to let me know when they understood or an obvious quizzical expression to express they hadn't. It was the type of nonverbal receipt I suggested waiting for earlier and was surprised by how gratifying it felt! In fact, it was one of the first times I had the satisfaction of feeling I'd really gotten through to every single person listening to me. If one of them gave me the slightest head tilt or confused look during the discussion, I found myself instinctively offering more information or repeating what I'd said in different words. Because I seldom get this kind of feedback talking to people with normal hearing, I'm especially grateful to this group for this valuable technique.

From that day on, I resolved to give everyone I was speaking with verbal or nonverbal feedback. I now nod when I understand what people have said to show I understand, and if I don't, I give them a more pronounced quizzical expression or say, "Excuse me, I want to make sure I understood you correctly. May I ask you to tell me that once again?" People truly appreciate it—and it's also a great way to cover it up if I catch my mind wandering!

I'm sure you've told something to coworkers or reports, and they simply stare at you with a blank expression. You want to rap on their foreheads and ask, "Hel-*lo*, is anybody there? Can you hear me? Are you understanding a word I'm saying?" Meanwhile your estimation of this person takes a nosedive.

When you show you don't quite understand something, people won't think you're slow. Conversely, they'll realize you're very wise for wanting the exchange to be completely clear.

Signal That You Understand (or Don't)

When a coworker is talking, the responsibility for clearly communicating is yours as well. Your colleagues, reports, and especially your boss, want to know if you've fully grasped what they've said—so help them out! In addition to clarity, this technique also makes you seem a lot smarter and reduces the possibility of later hearing, "It's a communication problem!"

26

Communicating in a Shrinking World

More and more workers have the opportunity to deal with fellow employees from around the world for whom English is a second language. It means that clear communication takes extra effort, but it's well worth it. Many people assume speaking another language is an either "they do" or "they don't" situation. That's far from the truth. Having struggled for decades trying to learn other languages (and mostly failing), I realize that many foreigners smile, nod, and pretend they understand just to be polite. Obviously you can't just say, "Hey, did ya *really* get it?" But there is something else you can do to communicate clearly, and the responsibility rests with you.

When people speak their own language at a normal speed, what they are saying often sounds like one long word to a foreigner. So the solution when dealing with ESL coworkers is really quite simple. Speak more slowly. Much more slowly. Excessively s-l-o-w-l-y. It may sound strange to you, but it won't to them. Not only will they understand what you've said; you'll make them proud of the fluency they've worked so hard to achieve.

LITTLE TRICK #29

Speak S-l-o-w-l-y for ESL Coworkers

At first, every foreign language sounds like gobbledy-gook. When conversing with someone whose mother tongue isn't English, slow your speaking down to an almost exaggerated level. Not only will the person want to communicate with you more, but there will be far fewer misunderstandings.

It goes both ways. If you don't understand a person due to her pronunciation, gently ask for clarification. Transmission and reception is what clear communication is all about, and as I've noted, that's not just up to the speaker.

Having said all that, let me now tell you about a possible exception—and it comes back to gender! There are times when no matter how clearly you've communicated, you just feel you haven't gotten through. Many women have told me this happens when trying to talk to males, and men say this same thing when talking with females. So let's explore that confounding communication conundrum next.

27

Talking to the Opposite Sex (Now *That's* a Foreign Language!)

Everyone knows men and women communicate differently. (If you have any doubt, I highly recommend Deborah Tannen's book, *Talking from 9 to 5: Women and Men at Work*.) But were you aware that the sexes listen differently, too? Please don't take what I'm about to say as an insult to either gender, because it's absolutely not. It's simply an observation on the diversity of listening styles. Both modes work fine when talking to someone of the same sex, but big problems come up trying to communicate to the other gender.

Women, you instinctively give "I got it" receipts when listening. In fact, many of you are like reassuring moms letting your kids know you understand. Even in adult conversations, you occasionally nod to let the speaker know you understood even if you don't agree. That's great. Keep using your responsive listening style when talking with a female colleague. She expects it. Afterward, of course, you are free to counter with your differing opinion, but at least she knows she got her point across.

Life isn't so easy for you when trying to communicate with men. I've heard women complain about a male colleague, "Talking to him is like talking to a nail!" My suggestion? Depending on the man you're talking to, tone down your little "I understand" signals. He's apt to think your nodding means you agree with him, even if you don't. Let him finish talking and then state your difference of opinion. If you'd listened to him female style, he'd think you're giving off mixed signals or worse—being erratic. The solution?

★ LITTLE TRICK #30

Women, Talking with a Male?
Listen Like a Male!

Ladies, when conversing with a man at work, switch to "guy-listening" style. If you nod to show you understand, he will rightfully (in the male way of communicating) think you agree. Then when you counter, he'll think you're inconsistent. I've heard men complain, "Women are erratic. They'll agree with you one minute and then change their minds." To avoid giving that impression, when talking with a man, *listen* like a man.

Gentlemen, when talking with another man, of course stick to your listening style. He knows where you're coming from because he uses the same comprehension signals (often, none). However . . .

★ LITTLE TRICK #31

Men, Talking with a Female? Listen Like a Female!

Gentlemen, when talking with a woman at work, even if you don't agree with her, signal that you understand what she's saying. A little nod goes a long way. Then, when she finishes, tell her your position even if it's dia-metrically opposed. At least she'll feel the two of you have *communicated*.

Here's a listening tip for both sexes when talking to customers. Nod understandingly while they're stating their objections and shower your customers with responses like "I see" or "I understand what you're saying." Now you look like you've fully taken your customer's needs into account and have come up with a solution to the problem. What is the solution? Whatever you're selling of course!

The communication conundrum isn't solved yet. Sometimes there's no language or gender barrier, but you're still not sure you've communicated clearly because your message was complicated. There's help coming.

28

How to Make Complicated Concepts Clear

Let's say you need to tell the temp filling in for the receptionist about her duties. Sounds simple. You inform her that she should make visitors feel welcome and answer the phone graciously. It's not rocket science.

Now let's say you work at NASA. You must tell a direct report the steps in accelerating the parabolic trajectory of autonomous aircraft while retaining zero-G experience. Not so simple.

But wait a minute! Depending on whom you're talking to, both directions are equally simple, or complicated. The NASA rocket scientist, whose head is usually above the clouds anyway, would be totally confounded by his duties as a receptionist. Being the scientist-engineer that he is, friendly casual conversation, either in person or on the phone, is a foreign language to him. And to the new receptionist, unless she has an advanced degree in aerospace engineering and physics, with experience in the constellation program featuring SRBs and Saturn V engines, the steps in accelerating the parabolic trajectory of autonomous aircraft while retaining zero-G experience would be, well, rocket science to her. You must be absolutely clear about how much your listeners already know—or don't—*before* explaining anything to them.

The ideas you must get across at work probably fall somewhere between telling a fill-in receptionist her duties and explaining parabolic trajectories to a rocket scientist. However, the bottom line is the same. Unless you've been working with someone for a very long time and are absolutely certain of the person's degree of knowledge, don't take chances with miscommunication at work.

I'm constantly on the lookout for new ways to help people communicate better. And since there's an app for everything now, I figured technology might have come up with something new. So I attended a convention where start-up entrepreneurs hoping for digital stardom could woo venture capitalists with their inventions. As I walked around the showcase space scanning the exhibits and banners, it seemed a few had come up with pretty cool ideas. I kept my fingers crossed that some high roller would hear their pitch and make their dreams come true. But hopes began to dwindle as I heard them talking to investors.

One booth advertised virtual assistant software to help companies with online customer service. I joined the small group gathered around the presenter, who was speaking too rapidly and using a lot of computer lingo. After a few minutes, one potential investor raised his hand, saying, "Excuse me, can you tell me exactly the difference between a chatbot and a virtual agent?"

"Well, that's pretty basic," the presenter chuckled. "I'll explain that later to you if you like." He then continued with his speed-of-light discourse, never once stopping to ask if the group understood or had questions. No doubt insulted by the put-down, that investor walked away, soon followed by others with confused expressions on their faces. I, too, left, figuring if the presenter didn't have the communication skills to handle the investor's question sensitively, how could he create software to communicate better with customers?

I didn't find a tech invention for better communicating that day. But I did indeed find something important— a reinforcement of how *not* to communicate and how *not* to explain a concept to coworkers so they understand it. It starts by not assuming anything! You must encourage feedback and get your listeners to ask questions. Employees don't like confessing ignorance in front of their colleagues, so make it easy for them. You might be hesitant to ask, "Did you understand?" fearing you'd be insulting their intelligence. But there are other ways to know if they really got it. Say things like . . .

- "I know that might sound confusing. Shall I tell you a little more about that aspect?"

- "That sounds very complicated. You must have questions."

- "I was really confused the first time it was explained to me. Please ask me anything."

- "Does that make sense? Please tell me."

- You could even feign a confession by saying, "I didn't explain that very well. May I try again or put it in other words?"

Now you're helping them save face while assuring they understood. Communicating clearly at work is too important to leave to chance!

If after answering questions, you still have lingering doubts that they got it, go a step further and have them repeat it back to you. Say something like, "Phew, I know that was a big information dump. Could I ask you to explain it back to me?

★ LITTLE TRICK #32

Press for Questions or Repetition

When talking to anybody about anything on the job, you must make absolutely sure your listeners understand precisely what you're saying. To do this, encourage questions or have them tell you what they think they heard. Make sure no one can blame a screw-up on "a communication problem" in your department.

Now let's turn our attention to another big challenge to communicating clearly—determining the right time to talk to someone, especially your boss.

29

Time Is Money,
Especially at Work

And top professionals spend theirs very carefully. No matter how important your question, or how pleasantly you approach a coworker to give or receive information, bad timing can mean bad results for you. If she's busy, she might listen just to be polite, but she won't take the time to really understand what you're saying. She might even give you an answer, but it's not a thought-out one because her mind was elsewhere. Business bloggers got wise to time commitments a long time ago. They preface their posts with "three-minute read," "four-minute read," etc. If it goes over five minutes, they leave off the time commitment. Good choice! Five minutes is an eternity when you're busy.

So how can you make sure your bosses and coworkers take time to listen and respond to you thoughtfully? By using a technique I've written about before and teach in all my communication seminars called the "Stoplight Technique." The name comes from the traffic signals you see on practically every corner in big cities. Red means, "Stop! Do not cross." Yellow says, "Oops, time is getting short. You better hurry." And green is, "Sure, no problem. Don't rush. Just amble on across." Some stoplights even give you the number of seconds you have left to cross and let you decide if you want to make a run for it or not.

Because time is money at work, most people know they shouldn't just plop down in someone's chair or telephone a coworker out of the blue to discuss something. They'll preface a conversation with, "Is this a good time to talk?" Or "Do you have a few minutes to talk?" But here's the problem. Even if the person says yes, you don't know whether he *really* has time to discuss the matter in depth now, or if he just wants you to quickly hit on the highlights.

You wouldn't dream of walking into a busy person's office, grabbing a heavy paperweight off her desk, and hurling it at the clock on the wall. When you invade her day, you're doing the same thing psychologically. And how much is she going to listen to you after you did that?

Here's where the "Stoplight Technique" comes to the rescue. A colleague who accomplishes more in a day than most people do in a week said he tells everyone in the company where he works that he doesn't want to disturb them at an inopportune time. So he asks his colleagues and bosses if he can start future conversations with an unusual question, "What color is your time?" He then explains that it's like a stoplight.

He says:

- "If you're really rushed, tell me you're *red.* Then I won't bother you now, but we'll find another time to talk when you're more relaxed."

- "If you say *yellow,* it means you're busy, but if it's quick, we can deal with it now."

- "And if you say *green,* it means, 'Sure, I've got time. Go ahead.'"

My friend told me his coworkers really loved the game, especially his boss, and it caught on at his company. Now practically everybody there uses it, and he said he senses less tension and feels communicating is clearer.

LITTLE TRICK #33

The Stoplight Technique

Introduce the "Stoplight Technique" at your company. I predict coworkers will appreciate it, especially bosses who feel constantly frustrated by interruptions. Ask if they'd like you to use it with them. I've never gotten a no, and you, too, will probably get an emphatic yes!

There's another time problem at work, and that's the nonstop talker. He or she goes on and on and on. You've heard of 12-step programs like Alcoholics Anonymous, Gamblers Anonymous, and Narcotics Anonymous? HR should establish one for employees with verbal diarrhea and call it "On and On Anonymous." Let's talk about that one next.

30

Shorter Is Sweeter— and Clearer

Whenever I ask a question in my seminars, most attendees give concise answers, but there's usually one in the group who refuses to stop talking. Some people are in love with the sound of their own voice. You've probably got one or two folks like that at your company.

I'll never forget one windbag at a client's company, where I attended several of their meetings. A team leader asked her group, "Have you had any particular challenges working on this project? Tucker, who'd apparently been with the organization a long time, cleared his throat and jumped in, "Well, as everyone knows, I don't like to start trouble, but . . ." One or two of his colleagues chuckled sardonically. It seemed Tucker loved an audience, and everyone knew it all too well. Pointing his finger in the air, he continued, "People never get back to me. I write e-mails to production, marketing, and sales, and no one ever answers my messages. I send out a second and a third one, and what do I get back? Nothing! So then I start calling around, but no one picks up the phone. So I try again and . . ."

Five minutes later, Tucker was still talking, and at this point, no one was capable of stopping the Tucker train. I sensed some were starting to blame the team leader for letting him waste their time and not reclaiming control of the meeting. Talkative individuals like Tucker may have the gift of gab, but when they go on too long, their gift turns into theft, theft of their listeners' valuable time.

Sitting there while he droned on, I wanted to say, "Tucker, don't you get it? The longer you continue, the less convincing you are. Can't you see that your colleagues are tuning out and blaming you for derailing the meeting? Don't be surprised if the next time, they leave you off the list of meeting invitees." Tucker could have made his point more effectively in one sentence by simply saying, "I'm having difficulty getting responses to my e-mails."

Whether you're speaking up in a meeting or just shooting the breeze in the break room, use what I call the "One-Minute Gag Rule."

The One-Minute Gag Rule

Set an imaginary timer when you start talking, and no matter how interesting your point, after one minute, invite someone else to get a word in. Look at one of your listeners and ask, "Aaron, what do you think?" Or "Vanessa, what's your view on that?" In other words, when time's up, hush up! If you make it a habit to give the floor to others, your colleagues will be more apt to listen when you start speaking again.

31

Kick But

I bet you thought that was a typo. Spelling it with two *t*'s, as in "kick butt," implies something quite different and is usually done by bosses. Here I'm referring to the simple coordinating conjunction "but." That word negates anything you said before it, especially the word "yes." People do that so often, it should be in the dictionary as one word, "yesbut." (Which really means "no.")

Here's a way around using the term. Let's say you've created a presentation for your team that you'll be sharing with colleagues in a meeting. You're proud of it, and in fact, it's so good, you'd like your boss to attend. Keeping your fingers crossed that he'll accept, you invite him. His immediate response is, "Yes, but I'll be out of town that day." He said it so fast you didn't even have the split second to enjoy his "yes" before he kicked you with "but" and you realized he really meant "no." Here are other examples I've heard bosses say:

Employee: "Do you think it's a good idea?"

Boss: "*Yes, but* we don't have time for that right now."

Employee: "Will you think about my request?"

Boss: "*Yes, but* we have a lot of other things to think about first."

Employee: "Did you like the report?"

Boss: "*Yes, but* it didn't cover what I asked."

Saying "but" so quickly contradicts "yes," and whatever follows is a punch in the gut. Wouldn't you have felt more supported by your boss if he'd said, "That's great and I'd really like to come to your presentation." Then paused before saying, "I will, *however*, be out of town." Do you sense the difference?

Say a colleague asks you for a favor and you must turn her down. Tell her . . .

"I'd love to help you with that project." *Pause.* "My workload is so heavy, *however,* that . . ."

"I wouldn't mind covering your station when you're at lunch on Wednesday." *Pause.* "*However*, I promised to have lunch with . . ."

"I'd be happy to introduce you to the CEO of my company." *Pause.* "I've introduced her to three people already this year, *however*, and . . ."

In these instances, you didn't start any sentences with "Yes, but," and you neatly tucked the soft negation into the middle of your next sentence. Good going!

LITTLE TRICK #35

Kick "But"

Avoid "but" by saying something pleasant and supportive. Make it a whole sentence with a period at the end. Then couch "however" in the middle of your next sentence. It makes the point that your answer is really no, and it maintains goodwill. Subtleties like this add up, making relationships on the job run more smoothly.

32

What's the Weather Got to Do with Success?

No matter how clearly you feel you've been communicating, I'm sure you've found times, as I have, when you just don't seem to get through to people. You've done everything right, but your words still don't seem to penetrate. A meeting goes wrong, people don't listen to your presentation, or you don't get a coveted assignment that you asked for so succinctly.

It's human nature to blame a failure on anyone but ourselves. I've heard employees grumble about not getting what they wanted due to an "unfair boss," "a bad-mouthing colleague," or a "personality conflict." They say they lost the sale because a "colleague undermined them," "someone gave them the wrong information," or the "delivery didn't come on time." The list goes on. But very few would have the guts to blame a personal failure on the weather like I'm going to do now—and science supports my position!

Several years ago, a company that was considering bringing me on as a consultant asked what day I could come to Texas to meet with the executives I'd be working with. We decided on a 3 p.m. meeting the following Thursday. My plane arrived in Dallas around noon, and I rented a car to go to the hotel. Later that afternoon, as I was leaving for the meeting, I peered up at dark thunderclouds rolling in. While driving to the company, thick sheets of rain pelted down on my car, and it felt like night. I turned on the windshield wipers, plowed through horrific traffic and lines of honking cars, and, by some miracle, arrived at the company's headquarters only seven minutes late.

Upon arrival, a brusque woman came down to the lobby to escort me to the conference room. There I was confronted by a long table full of scowling men and women leaning back with crossed arms. As I was being introduced, I saw by their expressions that their hopes of getting an early start home were dwindling. At the sound of each thunderclap, several glanced out the windows at the downpour. Not 20 minutes into the meeting, various attendees mumbled an apology and left the conference room, no doubt planning to make a dash for their cars. It was no surprise to me that I didn't get the gig.

Since then, I've run across research about weather affecting people's moods. Whether it's a business lunch, an interview, or a meeting, the weather can have a detrimental effect on any gathering. First, there's the lack of light on overcast or rainy days. Dark lighting cues the brain to manufacture melatonin, the sleep hormone.

Conversely, the sun triggers chemical brain reactions that make people more alert and will lift their moods. The best part, sunlight also produces serotonin, the feel-good hormone used in antidepressants. But there's no serotonin rush on cloudy days, just the opposite.

That Thursday was an unusually cold day for Texas, and low temperatures also have a negative effect on people's moods. Reduction in atmospheric pressure causes bodily fluids to move, which results in pressure on the nerves and joints, causing increased pain, stiffness, and reduced mobility. Your immune system tries harder to keep your body warm, so energy is directed toward those tasks, making you feel lethargic. If any of the executives in the meeting had a bad back, aching neck, or other chronic pain, it was surely acting up. Lousy weather sucks all the way around.

Since I became aware of the weather effect, I also notice I have more disappointing results with potential clients on gloomy days, and audiences are less responsive to my speeches. In short, on bad weather days, everything looks less desirable—your product, your service, even you.

So what's my tip for clear, successful communication? You obviously can't change the weather. However, if you have an important meeting, lunch appointment, presentation, interview, or conference coming up, check the weather forecast.

Schedule for Success

If the weather looks bad and it's possible, change your event to a nicer day. To increase your chances of a successful outcome, go for the most pleasant day of the week. If your event is slated for a drizzly, cold, dark day, reschedule if you can. It can make a difference, seriously.

Now let's talk about the next crucial success element, credibility. We'll deal with two kinds: one resides in the cloud (your online image) and the other in your company (your personal contact with people). You need total credibility in both, because when you become a leader, without it you won't be leading long.

PART IV

CREDIBILITY

33

The World Sees You as the Web Sees You — So Watch Out!

In the next year or so, you'll view or "meet" millions of people online, more than you could ever shake hands with in a lifetime. And some of these relationships will be more meaningful than your face-to-face professional contacts. People form an almost indelible first impression of you, often even before hearing your voice or meeting you in person. That means, for professional success, your web persona must be credible, consistent, and exceptional. Make sure everything you post matches the face you want to show the world.

Imagine, for a moment, you're strolling through a virtual world. You see people interacting with each other and advertising themselves based on their public online information. Some people look like they party for a living; others are dressed in business attire or walking with their kids. A few are casually chatting, and several are sitting alone. Looking around, you make some decisions. Whom would you talk to? Whom would you avoid? Whom would you run away from?

Let's say you go up to someone who is well dressed and has the same interests as you. But when you try to talk to her, you find her contact information entirely too confusing to make the effort to meet her, so you move on. She might have been your new boss or a great hire, but since she didn't make it easy to contact her, you'll never know.

And what about that guy who looked like a party animal? Perhaps he's a highly professional and intelligent candidate seeking a new job. But if you were the company president, would you reach out to party boy? You probably wouldn't go much beyond his supercasual image to discover he had an excellent education and work history. Even if you did research his qualifications, would his online persona look like he could do the job? Most people don't let their fingers dance across the keyboard long enough to find out.

What you put online must grab the right kind of attention and express what you want to communicate about yourself. Otherwise, people will click next or swipe left. If you don't brush up your web presence, you'll never know why you were passed over. Everyone makes judgments based on first impressions, and never before in history have your professional and personal lives overlapped on such a large scale. It means both your lives need to represent who you are to others online. If you only have a business persona, a potential employer would have to search further to pick a candidate who has interests similar to his or others on the team. But without a personal online presence, he couldn't find your hobbies, your everyday look, and other perhaps relevant information that wasn't in your business profile. And if you only have a personal persona, most potential employers can overlook you.

Your web presence should be sufficiently detailed to give a good understanding of your professional life, your personal interests to an extent, and have serious-sounding contact information readily available. Would serious professionals contact someone whose e-mail is koolkid420@gmail.com, bigstud@hotmail.com, or gannonfamily@aol.com? If you don't have a professional e-mail address, how could they give colleagues your contact information without getting laughed at? Now this presents a challenge if you have a common name like John Smith, of which there are 46,000. It's especially annoying if a famous person happens to have the same name as you!

What do you do to distinguish yourself? You may have to add your middle initial or that middle name you've always hated. You won't find many John Ebenezer Smiths! In the event that you don't have a middle name, you may have to resort to adding numbers to your e-mail address, JohnSmith46001@gmail.com.

Incidentally, if you haven't done so already, be sure to edit your social media profile addresses to something more professional that you wouldn't be embarrassed to share. Before a colleague chided me, I had the convoluted URL that LinkedIn gave me with a slew of numbers after my name. I'm sure she figured that if I didn't know how to change my profile address, I couldn't use more than basic e-mail applications either. (She was right at the time.)

LITTLE TRICK #37

Stalk Yourself Online

The first thing most people do when they want to find out more about an individual, whether for professional or personal reasons, is jump online. Beat them to it! Set aside an hour or two to search yourself online. Then fix anything you find that doesn't present the image you want.

How to Protect Your Online Image

A simple search online for your name can bring up a professional photo of you in front of a cheering crowd, proudly accepting an award for being the best in your field. But a few more clicks can then dig up a video of you beer-bonging on the beach with your buddies and passing out totally plastered. Disasters like this can happen, so check for privacy settings before posting.

LITTLE TRICK #38

Scrutinize Your Settings

This may be obvious to you (I hope it is), but I mention it here because you'd be surprised by how many employees forget to adjust their privacy settings and then wonder why they didn't get the promotion or new job. Make sure everything you want to keep private is *only* available to those you want to see it, and not just anyone with an Internet connection.

You've heard the saying "A picture is worth a thousand words." Well, people don't take the time to read a thousand words nowadays, but your online photo hits them in a flash. It's a priceless professional tool. Whenever a publisher wants my author picture for the back of one of my books, I agonize. What mugshot should I choose? The one with the toothy grin to look warm and friendly? Or the one with my mouth closed for a more thoughtful and introspective image? Should I wear makeup, or should I go for the more natural look (which means spending an hour in front of the mirror painting my face, so it looks like I'm not wearing makeup)?

Some professionals post the same photo on every site, which makes viewers wonder if it's the only one they have of themselves looking presentable. Post a primary photo for a consistent main image, but have a few others as well.

Be careful, though. I've seen expressions that make doctors look heartless, dentists look sadistic, leaders look weak, and employees look like they're posing for *Cosmopolitan* or *Muscle Man*. Before posting any picture, run it past a trusted colleague. Don't put anything out there you wouldn't want your boss to see. Facebook photos and comments have gotten many employees canned.

Now let's talk about your all-important credibility within the company's walls.

34

Truth or Consequences (the Consequences Can Be Huge)

Have you ever heard a colleague tell the boss that he was late due to an accident on the highway or that the doctor's appointment took longer than she'd planned? You knew they were lying because they'd previously joked with you about their oversleeping due to hangovers. Chances are the boss knew they were, too, because human bodies and faces make subconscious moves that reveal the truth. Every expression and bodily movement that accompanies your words reveals the "real" you and what you're thinking at the moment.

Maybe you sensed your boss was lying when she said there was a hiring freeze this quarter or gave you a much earlier completion date for a project. You probably didn't speak up, but there was something in her manner that made you doubt her. So the next time she told you, "There's no truth to those layoff rumors," you were on guard. After mistrusting somebody once, whatever he or she says the next time has far less credibility. There comes a point when even the person's white lies sound like whoppers to you.

Try never to let even the smallest lie creep into your communication, because if you're caught in one exaggeration, once being less than forthright, one teensy fib, your credibility starts to crumble. The better you recognize coworkers' microexpressions and body language discrepancies, the more skilled you become maneuvering your way through the corporate jungle. Abraham Lincoln is credited with saying, "You can fool all the people some of the time, and some of the people all the time. But you cannot fool all the people all the time." Having said that . . .

Everybody Lies

Most people a little, some a lot. All employees occasionally equivocate, embellish, or take liberties with the facts. Research tells us a whopping 22 percent of fibs at work are about something an employee did or didn't do that the boss wouldn't like. Or boasting that an as-yet-unfinished assignment was already done.

If you've ever been guilty of this, you've got a lot of company. But be careful; a tiny fib today could screw up your career big-time tomorrow. Even one untruth establishes that you take liberties with the facts. There is an oft-told story that Prime Minister Winston Churchill once asked a socialite, "Madam, would you sleep with me for 5 million pounds?"

The demure socialite responded, "Oh, my goodness, Mr. Churchill . . . That's shocking . . . Well, I mean . . . I suppose . . . We would have to discuss terms, of course . . ."

Churchill, smiling, then asked, "Would you sleep with me for 5 pounds?"

The shocked socialite gasped, "Mr. Churchill, what kind of woman do you think I am?"

Churchill replied calmly, "Madam, we've already established what you are. Now we are merely haggling about price."

Once caught in a lie, no matter how minuscule it is, the teller is labeled a liar.

How to Avoid Being Suspected of Lying

Why did you feel your boss wasn't being truthful about the hiring freeze or layoffs? Because you, like everyone else, are a human polygraph machine. Yet a lie-detector machine is nothing more than a mechanical apparatus measuring fluctuations in the autonomic nervous system, such as changes in breathing patterns, heartbeat, blood pressure, sweating, and other signs of emotional arousal. Are polygraphs accurate? That's arguable, but the FBI, police forces, and many companies use them for their life-or-death games of truth or consequences.

What is not arguable, however, is that when people are lying, physical changes take place in their bodies. The naked eye may not be able to pick up on the changes, but internal variances cause us to make unconscious movements we might not otherwise.

One of my consulting clients has an excellent sales manager named Logan. Every member of his sales team consistently comes in over quota, and there isn't a slacker among them. I once congratulated him and said, "Logan, I don't know how you do it. Every last one of your salespeople is tops. How do you find them?" Then joking, I asked, "Have you ever hired a lemon?"

He replied, "No, not really, Leil. I've been very lucky."

"Come on, Logan," I protested, "It's a lot more than luck. You have a keen eye for talent."

He shrugged and said, "Well, I don't know about that. But after all these years, I've gotten pretty good at telling if any of my reports or a job candidate is lying."

"So what's your secret?" I nagged.

His face got serious, and he said, "I just watch people as they're talking." My questioning expression encouraged him to continue. "Well, for example, just last month I was interviewing a candidate for a sales job. He sounded pretty confident and had a lively personality. I felt he was perfect for making cold calls like our sales force has to do. I then asked the young man why he was applying for this particular job. He looked me straight in the eyes and said, 'It gives me a sense of pride when I complete a sale and provide a good service to a new customer.'

"I liked his answer," Logan continued, "so I asked him if, due to all of the changes in methods of communication now, he thought cold calling was dead. He sounded excited and was still totally relaxed, answering, 'Oh, no, a lot of conditions in sales can change, but connecting with people never does. When I contact potential buyers, I always keep it focused on the customer and the value the product can provide.'

"That sounded good to me," Logan said. "So I asked him why he left his previous job. At that point, the candidate's eyes darted away fleetingly before regaining eye contact. Then, I saw his fingers curling as though starting to make a fist. He took his arm off the chair, rubbed the back of his neck, and at one point while he was talking, he put a hand up to his mouth.

"With words my candidate was telling me he felt his 'growth opportunities were limited' in the previous company. But his body was telling me another story. I started suspecting he wasn't telling me the real reason he left. Of course, just that one episode of fidgeting wouldn't prove he was a liar. However, it was enough that I decided to revisit the subject.

"To test his 'baseline' personality, I went back to a subject I knew he'd like and asked him to tell me about his strengths. Again he relaxed and rested an arm on the back of the chair. Without batting an eye, he told me he was a good listener so he could better undestand customer needs. He leaned back, saying he prided himself on being a persuasive speaker. I agreed that he was."

"I still couldn't put my finger on it," Logan repeated, "but I continued to feel something was wrong. So in different words I returned to why he left his previous position. I asked, 'Was the fact that you didn't see any opportunities to grow the only reason you left?' At that, he once again shifted his weight, momentarily looked away, and then started rubbing his forearm.

"Before that second round of fidgeting movements, I was about to hire him right there on the spot. I'm glad I didn't, though, because I later contacted some people at his old company and discovered he'd been a real troublemaker and had nasty disagreements with his previous sales manager." Logan had trapped his liar!

I'll put the following suggestions in the form of dos and don'ts so you can avoid suspicion when you're talking with people at work. If you're stressed by a question, the instinct is to speak faster and louder as though driving that point home. So if the subject changes to something touchy while you're talking, concentrate on keeping your same speed and volume. If you don't, they'll sense you're getting tense about something and will be on extra lookout. Also be careful your voice doesn't crack, and avoid repetitive throat clearing or coughing, which can also flag a fib. Don't break eye contact or close your eyes when responding to a question, and avoid hesitating or prefacing your response with "uh."

When a person's words say one thing and his body says another, science calls it a "disconnect." I'm sure you've had a gut feeling you should reject an offer or say yes to a suggestion, and yet you had no real evidence of *why* you felt that way. You just had a hunch, and hunches are very real. Dozens of studies like "Just a Hunch: Accuracy and Awareness in Person Perception," published in the *Journal of Nonverbal Behavior*, proved how reliable they really are.

★ LITTLE TRICK #39

Fight Fidgeting

When the discussion really counts, ignore your itching nose, prickling foot, tingling ear, or sweating neck. Above all, keep your hands away from your face; it could look like you're "hiding" a lie. Make sure your voice is smooth and speaks at the same speed throughout, especially when the conversation turns troublesome. When answering important questions, keep good, but not exaggerated, eye contact. Feeling your body itch, prickle, tingle, or sweat is a heck of a lot less unpleasant then being suspected of lying.

It's not just lies when speaking. An online lie can be professional suicide. With e-mail and chat applications, the days of "he said–she said" (and "he said–he said" and "she said–she said") are in the past, Your every word is forever in the cloud. You write something, and at the drop of a forwarded message, the whole company knows whatever it is.

Teensy Fibs Are OK, Right?

Wrong! No matter how minuscule the lie, it matters, because it puts everyone on red alert for more. For instance, let's say at 9:50 you receive a text from Tom asking, "Can we talk?"

You text back, "I've got a meeting at 10, but sure, go ahead and call me." Tom calls, and to your surprise, he wants to talk about a subject that's important to you, so when 10:05 rolls around, you're still talking. Tom's thinking, "Wait a minute; he said he had a meeting at 10. That's great, I guess he's going a little over time for me." But now it's 10:15 and you're *still* talking. This time Tom is suspicious and thinks, "Hey, that meeting must have been B.S. because he still talking to me." Lie alert!

OK, Tom may not accuse you of lying, but you lose a little credibility in his eyes, and so the next time you talk, he's on the lookout for lies. Tiny untruths add up, and when the pile gets high enough, your credibility topples.

35

Another Integrity Wrecker

Unless you are extremely experienced at lying, which I hope, for your sake, you're not, controlling minor movements of annoyance is difficult. Even if you are being 100 percent truthful, any pain or physical discomfort can cause you to *look* like you're lying.

An assistant was once helping me with research for one of my books, and I was anxiously awaiting the names of some studies I'd asked her for. But Charlene, looking glum, told me a computer glitch had deleted the information she'd gathered. While explaining this to me, she was constantly moistening her lips with her tongue, which made her look nervous. I happened to have a small tube of lip gloss in my purse and asked if she'd like some. "Oh yes, Leil," she said. "Thanks so much. I got sunburned at the beach last weekend, and my lips are killing me."

Aha, retroactively I understood why she kept moistening them with her tongue, and I felt sorry I'd mistrusted her. If Charlene had told me about the sunburn problem earlier, I would have been sympathetic and known the reason for it.

A similar thing happened once while I was consulting. An employee named Nick was proudly telling his boss, my client, that he was very close to making his quota this month. But he kept rubbing the back of his neck while talking and occasionally tilted his head to crack it. I remember my client looking askance at him and being a bit sarcastic about Nick's boast as though she didn't believe him.

Later that afternoon, I was casually chatting with Nick in the hall, and he was doing the same thing, rubbing and cracking his neck. I asked if it hurt. "Yes," he groaned, "last week I suffered whiplash and have to keep rubbing my neck to ease the pain." Now I understood why he had looked so uncomfortable in the earlier meeting. The next time I met with my client, I made it a point to tell her about his whiplash and that he had to rub his neck often because it hurt. I hoped she would understand retroactively and not think his movements were due to fibbing.

Not lying at work is crucial to your credibility, but you must also avoid the *appearance* of telling an untruth. If any physical discomfort makes you rub, scratch, twitch, twist, massage yourself, or make any other unusual movements, find a way to casually allude to it so no one thinks it's a nervous lying signal. If only Nick had mentioned his whiplash to his boss and Charlene had told me about her sunburned lips, they wouldn't have been suspect.

★ LITTLE TRICK #40

Give a Heads-Up on What Hurts

Of course you don't want to sound like a kvetch, but if you have any physical discomfort that causes you to make nervous gestures, casually mention it before or right after the first episode. Appearing trustworthy is a top priority for you at work, and you must never give anyone the slightest suspicion that you're lying.

Here's a scary thought. Even if you are not lying, your body can display similar physiological reactions if the person you're talking with intimidates you in any way—like your boss! So be *extra* wary at those times.

36

When a Little Lie
Is Unavoidable

OK, now that I've gotten on a soapbox and preached that you should never lie, even the most honest employee knows that telling the occasional white lie or downplaying certain facts (or, shall we say, "tweaking reality") is sometimes the most prudent choice. Perhaps you need to protect someone from hearing a negative truth or cover for a deeply revered colleague. For strategic purposes, leaders must sometimes exaggerate their vision for the success of their company or omit information they feel is fear-inducing or harmful. Almost everyone must occasionally take a few liberties with the truth for justifiable reasons.

I hope you don't have to fib, but be aware that some professionals like FBI agents and criminal investigators (maybe even your boss) resort to a very common liar-trapping technique. They may ask you to give an exceptionally lengthy chronological description of events, because they want to hear all the details to see if something "doesn't fit." Here is a suggestion for those trying times.

Are you aware of the tool that sports psychologists employ called visualization? Olympic champions use it to perform their best. In their mind's eye they "see" themselves in action, their bodies twisting, bending, flipping, and flying to get the gold. Skiers "hear" the wind racing past their ears, divers "listen to" the deafening splash of the water, and javelin throwers "watch" the projectile hurtling through the air at the speed of sound. They envision the entire sequence before moving a muscle.

Visualization is not just for top-level competitive athletes. It's for anyone who wants to achieve their goals and convince others of something. Don't just rehearse your story; *visualize* it. When you picture something intensely, repetitively, and sequentially in your mind, it brings it closer to reality. So the, hopefully few times you deem it best to tweak the truth, take a tip from Olympic athletes.

★ LITTLE TRICK #41

"See" Your Story

Relive what you must tell others step-by-step in your mind's eye. Employ all your senses to experience the truth as you must tell it. See the colors; hear the sounds; feel the temperature. Then replay the mental "video" over and over in your mind to bring it to life.

Just in case, when it really counts, run the story in your mind backward, too. Top investigators sometimes ask suspects to recount what happened in reverse order.

(Hmm, did I hear you just ask if this chapter should be titled, "How to Lie"? No, it should not!)

What are the times it's most tempting to lie at work? Well, the most common by far is when you're late. The next chapter tells you how handle that.

37

When You're Late to Work

Getting out of bed early in the morning Monday through Friday sucks, but you don't dare hit snooze one more time or it could spell disaster. It's hell pulling your head off the pillow; pointing your nose toward the bathroom, then the closet, then the kitchen; and finally starting your commute. But, ahh, sometimes you just can't resist drifting into dreamland again. Until it hits you—*you're going to be late*! As they throw on their clothes, most employees' minds race for justifications. Lost car keys? Flat tire? Fluid leaks? Dead battery? No, bosses have heard them all, and if you give a flimsy excuse, you risk being labeled a liar.

When you first realize you're going to be late, text or e-mail your boss immediately, but *don't* give an excuse now unless it's catastrophic. Do, however, say what time you're planning to be there. Most managers tell me they really don't care why an employee is late; they just want to know what time he or she will arrive and that it won't happen again. If your job requires someone to be on duty promptly to answer the phone or work a piece of equipment, arrange for a fill-in. If you can't, tell your boss you'll work late or through lunch to make up for the lost time.

Of course, walking in late leaves another conundrum, being faced with a room full of fish-eyed colleagues glaring at you questioningly. Now's the time to use a technique similar to Little Trick #1, "Your Daily Grand Entrance." Look relaxed and proud, like you were coming from a meeting with the president who'd just promoted you. Then go right to your desk and dive into work. Of course, be sure to thank the colleague who covered for you using Little Trick #15, "Prolong Your Praise" and add, "Anytime I can do the same for you, I'd be more than happy to."

When You're Late to a Meeting

There's always one person who slinks in after it's begun, right? The tardy employee's natural inclination is to creep in with a mortified expression and blurt out an immediate excuse. You've heard them all: "The traffic was terrible." "My dentist appointment ran late." "I had to take my kid to the doctor" or "pet to the vet."

Don't demean yourself that way! You needn't crawl in like a panting dog brandishing an excuse between his teeth.

A gracious "Excuse me" suffices at first. Then just proceed promptly and proudly to your seat as though you had been the first to arrive. (Don't worry; you'll nonchalantly sneak your excuse in later.)

I once witnessed the perfect execution of this technique in a meeting while consulting for Wilson Windows. The president scheduled a 9 a.m. Monday morning meeting to discuss a potential new product with his team. He especially wanted the input of his new designer, Courtney Carr. But Courtney was nowhere to be seen. He delayed the proceedings for about five minutes and then, obviously exasperated, started without her. About 9:30 Courtney glides in, completely composed. She mouthed a simple "Please excuse me" to the group and found a seat. I'm sure everyone was thinking, "Well, la-di-da. What's *her* excuse." With a steely expression Wilson gave her a cold, "Welcome Ms. Carr."

About 10 minutes later, Courtney raised her hand with a question. She prefaced it with, "I apologize if this was answered before. I missed the first part of the meeting because my mother had a bad fall in the bathroom, and I had to take her to the doctor." I saw a few compassionate looks on the other employees' faces. Then, without missing a beat, she proceeded with her query about the new product. Cool.

After the meeting, several of the employees and I went to Courtney's area to express our sympathy. As we were talking, Mr. Wilson came in saying, "Oh, Courtney, I'm terribly sorry about your mother. I hope she'll be OK, and if you need to leave early, just let me know." Obviously, Courtney had more than rectified herself in her boss's and colleagues' eyes.

Thank heaven, usually the reason you're tardy won't be as dire as Courtney's. Maybe it's a hackneyed one like "My car wouldn't start," "I had a miserable headache," or "My kids were acting up." In these cases, I suggest you do not reveal the reason right now. Instead try this tactic.

Enter gracefully with a "Please excuse me" to everyone. (Don't just direct this to the boss, because that sounds servile.) Then take your seat with grace and think of a question you can ask later. A short time into the proceedings, use Courtney's apology about missing the first part of the meeting. That shows you're not trying to cover up your tardiness. If it's an extreme excuse like Courtney's, mention it now. If not, substitute, "And if you ask me later, I'll be happy to share the unfortunate details with you." Then immediately follow up with your question. Chances are that no one will ask you the reason later. If someone does, of course, tell the truth.

The beauty of this technique is twofold. One, you come off as completely confident and not trying to hide anything. And two, you must only reveal your flimsy excuse to the people who ask! And most won't.

LITTLE TRICK #42

The Deferred Excuse

When late to a meeting, make a poised entrance accompanied by a simple "Excuse me," and that's it—for now. Later, ask a question, saying you may have missed that part because you were late, and invite anyone to ask you about it later.

Next we'll talk about retaining your credibility, maintaining your self-respect as well as your boss's, and keeping your reputation as an honorable person intact—when you've totally screwed up!

38

Come Out Smelling Like a Rose When You're Guilty as Heck

Worst-case scenario: You are guilty as accused. Your superior knows it and is really pissed! Never fear—I'll give you a technique that I've written about before and teach in all my classes because it works exquisitely. Don't expect to be acquitted of the crime, but you'll come out smelling like a rose, sometimes even more fragrant than before you were caught.

When I was a preteen, I was infatuated with Wonder Woman. The cartoonist wrote that "she had the speed of Hermes, the wisdom of Athena, the strength of Hercules, and the beauty of Aphrodite." She could spin her arms around faster than the speeding bullets aimed at her and deflect them with her supercool silver bracelets. "PING!" "POW!" "ZAP!" And her thigh-high red boots were to die for.

My real-life Wonder Woman would be Wanda, who works at a manufacturing firm. The company president calls himself J.D. (Some big bosses feel cool using their initials as a first name.) During their weekly one-on-one, J.D. said he was disappointed in the product that one of the company's suppliers produced. "Wanda, I want you to tell Walter at Wonderful Widgets that I'm canceling his contract, effective immediately, and to disregard all future orders because his product is not up to par. I want no future contact with this man!"

Wanda was disappointed because she'd worked with Walter for years, and they'd become professional friends. But she did as she was told and wrote him an apologetic message explaining that her boss had asked her to terminate the contract.

A week later J.D. stuck his blood-red face out of his office and shouted to Wanda, "Get in here *now!*" Full of fury, he barked at her, "Walter just called acting like everything is hunky-dory and offered a 5 percent discount on our next order. Didn't you write, telling him that his contract is canceled and to disregard all future orders because his product is not up to par? And that I don't want any more contact with him?"

Most earthlings facing this frontal attack would have hemmed and hawed, explaining they wrote him but didn't, umm, put it precisely in those words. But not my Wonder Woman. With the speed of Hermes, the wisdom of Athena, and the strength of Hercules, Wanda calmly looked him straight in the eyes and replied: "J.D., I'm glad you brought that up. You are absolutely right. I told him you'd asked me to cancel the contract, but I didn't tell him 'to disregard all future orders because his product is not up to par.' Or that you 'don't want any more contact with him.' I now realize the misunderstanding that my not using your precise words has caused. I assure you it will never happen again."

Did you notice all the cool moves Wanda made in just a few sentences? Let's take those moves one by one:

> **"J.D., I'm glad you brought that up. You are absolutely right."** This crafty opening convinced her boss that the question didn't cow her. In fact, she used his name calmly and said she welcomed his bringing it to her attention. This stroked his ego nicely.

> **"I told him you'd asked me to cancel the contract, but I didn't tell him 'to disregard all future orders because his product is not up to par.' Or that you 'don't want any more contact with him.'"** Good going, Wanda. You gave a full confession. No hedging. No mincing words. You used your accuser's *precise* phrasing, which is what made your confession spectacular.

> **"I now realize the misunderstanding that my not using your precise words has caused."** That showed total insight and comprehension of what she did wrong.

> **"I assure you it will never happen again."** Here Wanda displayed that she is a responsible employee he could trust.

If You Really Want to Explain Yourself

This last step is optional—and sometimes you come out smelling sweeter if you don't use it. However, if you choose to, do the following. My Wonder Woman did, so she continued . . .

"Sometime, if you like, I'll share what my thinking was at the time." Notice she didn't anxiously say she wanted to explain immediately. J.D. seemed open to listening to her though, and so she continued . . .

"My thinking was that we should retain Walter's goodwill in case we ever needed him in the future. I now realize that caused the problem." That clarified her rationale, and Wanda presented it nondefensively.

"Thank you, J.D., for giving me the opportunity to explain my reasoning." Beautiful! I hope you never have to use it, but if you do, here is the seven-step confession that puts you miles above the average employee.

★ LITTLE TRICK #43

The Extraordinary Verbatim Confession

1. Tell your boss you're glad that she brought it up and that she is absolutely right.

2. Confess, using your boss's words *verbatim*. If she said you "stole" something, don't just confess to

"taking it." If she said you "forgot," don't just confess to "not remembering." No mincing words.

3. Acknowledge that you understand the problem it's caused and apologize.

4. Assure her it will never happen again.

5. Only at this point should you ask if she'd like to hear your reasoning.

6. If she does, explain your reason nondefensively.

7. Finally, thank her for the opportunity to share it.

This makes your boss realize she's dealing with a very special employee, and your confession will floor her—which is the proper position for her to kiss your hot red boots.

Now let's talk about another type of credibility, showing you really know your stuff. Making presentations is a must for that. The closer you get to the top, the more crucial it will be—and the more you'll have to make. Presenting by teleconference, videoconference, podcast, online, or virtual media is daunting, but the scariest of all is being in a room or assembly hall standing in front of your boss and coworkers. Everyone in the group is looking at you, awaiting your words of wisdom.

39

Make Presentations
to Gain Credibility

Facing legions of coworkers and perhaps your boss mainlines terror into the veins of the most fearless employees. I know all too well, because I was petrified of speaking to groups. The very thought of it turned my knees to jelly. So how did my worst fear become one of my greatest pleasures? It's a strange story and far too long to tell here. But for reasons that I may explain in another book, I embarked on an extensive, expensive, and exhausting journey to learn everything I could about public speaking. Toastmasters, the National Speakers Association, and individual coaches were a great help. But my biggest surprise was that, eventually, addressing audiences of sometimes thousands thrilled me. I was so passionate about it that I started conducting presentation skills seminars around the country. Now, looking back, I realize how much easier and faster it would have been if someone had given me the few tips I want to share with you now about making presentations.

Planning Your Presentation

Most people begin the process by thinking through their material. They make a list of what they must cover, figure out how long they'll have, and maybe what technology to incorporate. Makes sense, right?

No, you're getting way ahead of the game! In fact, the first step has nothing to do with your topic. Nor your presentation method. Nor your technology. Nor how you'll come across. Not even your handouts or how you'll dress. It's all about the *attendees*, the people in your audience. Ask yourself: Who are they? What do they know? What are they expecting? What do they want to learn about my subject? Then consider the following, because each has a surprising effect on the success of your overall presentation.

What time am I presenting? Often you don't have a choice, but if you do, go for mid-morning around 10, and here's why. If you present much earlier, latecomers who didn't get enough sleep will stagger in and nod off. Others will be frustrated, wanting to start their own work. If your talk is too close to lunchtime, attendees with grumbling stomachs start looking at their watches. A good second choice is mid-afternoon, but not right after lunch nor the end of the day. If they had dessert, a sugar rush makes them sleepy after lunch. (When I give full-day seminars that include lunch, I ask the convention hall to hold off on dessert and serve it later as an afternoon pick-me-up.) Definitely don't present at day's end. If you do, you risk facing something like my Dallas disaster, with attendees looking at their watches and itching to head home.

Where am I presenting? The venue will most likely be chosen. Keep in mind, though, that you must match your movements and volume to fit the size of the space. Make your gestures slightly larger than normal in the front of a conference room, and much larger than life in a huge room or auditorium. Actors tell sad stories of popular off-Broadway shows bombing when they went to Broadway just because they didn't adjust gestures to be seen from the back of the theater. If you don't have a microphone, pretend you're talking to someone in the last row, so everyone can hear.

How will they be seated? You may wonder why this counts, but it does, big-time. If it's not a conference room or auditorium with stationary seating, ask that chairs be arranged in one of these three ways:

- *Theater style* is the usual. But be sure to leave an aisle between every eight or nine chairs across for easy access to seats.

- *Chevron*, named after military officers' insignias, is a wide V-shape with an aisle down the middle. This is often my choice for long rooms, because participants can look toward each other more easily, which creates a friendlier atmosphere.

- *Semicircle* encourages interaction, but it might be too touchy-feely for corporate programs. Depending on your topic and goal, however, semicircle gives your presentation a more intimate feel. Just be aware, mostly male audiences can be uncomfortable with it.

What gender are the participants? The reason this makes a difference is because primarily female audiences interact more and like asking questions during Q and A. Males, not so much, especially in strict hierarchical companies. When presenting to an audience that consists primarily of males, I judge their mood and sometimes whisper in the president's ear, half-jokingly, "Your employees may peek at you to see if you're enjoying the presentation, so if you are, please show it." If the head honcho at your company is grumpy, consider doing what I did, or the response to your presentation could suffer through no fault of your own.

What is the audience's mood at that moment? As you're standing in front of them, don't start speaking immediately. Take a moment to look around the room to see the faces and pick up on their states of mind. How are they feeling? What are they expecting? What are they thinking about? Are they anxious about anything? If I'd picked up on the concerned mood around the conference table in Dallas, I could have done damage control with my first words. In fact, the biggest bomb I ever laid in front of an audience was because I didn't sense the mood of my listeners.

An investment company booked me for an evening address at its annual convention to encourage networking with executives from other parts of the country to learn best practices. I was the first speaker, and as I entered the hall, the meeting planner, Marina, was off to the side talking solemnly with several other people. I bounded up to them and asked who was going to introduce me. They looked at each other, and then Marina mumbled, "Uh, Leil, after everyone's arrived, just go up and start." That's peculiar, I thought, because after the president's or chairman's opening address, I'm usually introduced before I go on.

At the scheduled time, I walked energetically up to the stage with a big smile. As I often start my networking talks, I cheerfully asked them to stand up, find someone they didn't know, shake hands, and introduce themselves. A deafening silence hovered over the room and no one made a move. A few people woodenly stood up, but seeing they were alone, they gratefully slumped back into their seats. Dread set in as my eyes swept across a sea of deadpan expressions.

The next sound I heard was Marina rushing up behind me whispering, "Come with me, Leil." She whisked me into the hall and told me that, at the close of trading that day, their stock had taken the largest single drop in the company's history. Ouch, I didn't read the mood of the group and gladly offered to return my fee. Always pause, look over the people in your audience, and pick up on their "vibes" before opening your mouth.

40

Professional Speakers' Secrets

'm sure you've heard it from others, and I'll echo it: the secret is "Just be yourself." I know, I know, that seems impossible facing a room full of expectant eyes. But in my presentation skills seminars, I "trick" my students into being themselves. Here's how.

I first ask participants to think about something they're passionate about, perhaps a favorite sport, hobby, or exciting experience they've had. Then I ask each to tell the class about it in four minutes or less. As the students talk about their passion at the front of the room, I see their eyes light up, their voices echo excitement, and their hands gesture vigorously as though interpreting for the deaf. The other students, their audience, usually applaud enthusiastically and sincerely. Why? Because the speakers are being themselves, having fun, and are full of enthusiasm about the subject.

I then tell them to talk about the material they must present at work with the same exuberance, the same energetic expressions, the same large gestures. The result is astounding! Whatever the speaker is now talking about seems engrossing—and that's what makes an exciting presentation.

★ LITTLE TRICK #44

Present with Passion—Your Style

The next time you're enthusiastically talking with friends, have an out-of-body experience and watch yourself. Notice your gestures. Listen to the excitement in your voice. Then, when talking to your corporate audience about your topic, copy the same zeal and expansive gestures. That's the real you presenting at your best.

A Few Tricks of the Trade

Here are a few professional speakers' tips:

- Before presenting, avoid dairy products like cream in your coffee, because it creates excessive phlegm. (Also, though I have no idea why, many speakers swear by eating a green apple before speaking.)

- Just before your talk, find a private place to do Little Trick #3, "Make Your Bubble Bigger." It frees up your body for larger gestures and also helps shoo the butterflies out of your stomach.

- For nervous dry mouth, do what professional speakers do; they rub a little Vaseline on their teeth so their lips don't stick to them due to dry mouth.

- Be the first to arrive wherever you're presenting. Then stand in the same space to get comfortable with the lighting, the temperature, the noise from other offices, etc. You don't need any surprises while presenting.

- Unless it's a speech for a large audience, welcome or chat with attendees individually as they enter.

- After being introduced or called upon, walk *briskly* to where you're presenting—not sluggishly like someone's dragging you there unwillingly. (Some motivational speakers run to the stage, which I think is overdone.)

- As I said in the previous chapter, don't start talking the moment you're facing your audience. Pause; make eye contact to connect with the attendees. Only then, begin.

- When talking about material projected on a screen, don't turn 180 degrees to look at it. Indicate it with your hand while maintaining eye contact with the audience. Your face and body are presenting, not your back.

- Don't forget to have a glass of lukewarm, not cold, water within easy reach.

- While speaking, make sure your eyes meet briefly with as many audience members as possible. Even if the light is in your eyes and you can't see their faces, they won't know the difference. With large audiences, pretend you're an airline pilot scanning the horizon.

- To show confidence, step out from behind the podium if there is one, so your audience sees your entire body.

- If you need notes (we all do), jot a few in large writing to remind you of your next segment. If you must read from notes, occasionally glance down but keep your eyes mostly on your audience.

- The only parts of your presentation to memorize are your opening and closing lines. The rest of the time, stay in the moment so you can read your audience while speaking.

How to Cover Humiliating Bloopers

We're all afraid of screwing up, but if you're prepared with a few quips, it can sometimes endear you to the audience.

Professional speakers keep a dossier of "save lines." Here are a few of my favorites:

- If your joke falls flat, say, "Pretend it was serious."

- If you lose your train of thought, say, "Sometimes silence says a lot, but not this time." Or ask the audience, "What was I saying?" When someone reminds you, say, "Oh good, I'm glad someone was listening."

- The room is too hot? "I tried to lower the thermostat, but it's already melted."

- Too cold? "Frostbite medical pamphlets are available at the back of the room."

- There's a sudden big noise from outside the room? Tell the audience, "That's what we do to people who try to escape my talk."

- Oops, you belch or burp? Say, "Now that moves us to the topic of nonverbal communication."

- If you audibly pass gas, grab a pen, and, pretending to write, say, "That reminds me. Pay the gas bill."

- If you get a tough question you can't answer, say, "Ask me that at the break, and I'll avoid answering it then, too." (Be sure they don't take you seriously!)

The best way to get good at presenting is to give lots of talks to anyone who will listen. You can practice at PTA, social meetings, clubs, or any other gatherings. Addressing groups of people gets easier and each presentation is a little better than the last. You may even come to love speaking like I did!

41

Convincing Coworkers to See Things Your Way in Meetings

The following is so true I want to shout it from the rooftops and sing it from the skies. Whether it's a formal presentation, a meeting, or just a one-on-one conversation, two of the most important ingredients are passion and the power of stories. When I later run into people who say they enjoyed my speeches, they often mention one of the stories I told. They remember those more than the facts! If you use a tale to make your point, you grab your listeners' attention and guide their thinking.

One of my clients, Bruno Cucelli, the CEO of an upscale dress shirts designer, invited me to a meeting with his management team, five men and one woman, Danica. The group was discussing Danica's suggestion of adding a line of more casual shirts. Cucelli's line was conservative, and the men (who were on the older side) were obviously not supportive of Danica's suggestion.

One of them somewhat belligerently stated, "The company has no experience in the casual market." A second shrugged, "There are so many other casual shirt manufacturers out there, and we have no unique selling proposition." A third grumbled, "Kids don't recognize quality if it was staring them in the face." Although she hadn't spoken yet, Danica listened carefully and gave the impression she agreed with what her colleagues were saying.

At one point, she leaned forward, looked around the room, and glanced at each warmly. Then she started telling a story that had nothing to do with shirts. She began, "We're all old enough to remember Blockbuster video, right?" One or two of the men chuckled because they were all over 50 and remembered the disastrous death of that video rental business. She laughed and told them how thrilled she was when Blockbuster opened its doors. With excitement in her voice, she said, "It was terrific because the TV schedule no longer made me stay home to watch my favorite program that showed old movies." Making a wide gesture with her arms, she exclaimed, "They had a huge selection of films, and before Blockbuster, I had to pay exorbitant prices for the videotape if I wanted to watch a movie more than once. But when Blockbuster came in, I could see it as many times as I wanted to for just a few dollars. Their business model was beautiful," she continued excitedly. "After customers had rented a particular tape a few dozen times, it started yielding 100 percent profit for Blockbuster."

The men had no idea why she was telling this story, but her dramatic narrative and vivid gestures engrossed them. When she finished, however, they were confused. Finally, one of the executives articulated what they all were thinking, "Danica, what does the Blockbuster debacle have to do with our shirts?"

Her smile told me that was precisely the question she'd been waiting for. Her face became serious as she told the group, "More than half the workforce is now millennials, and hardly any of them wear dress shirts to work." To break the tension, she joked. "Oh, there's still a very strict dress code. My nephew works in Silicon Valley and says employees are practically ostracized if they don't wear a T-shirt."

She then placed two articles she'd found online on the table facing her boss. One was from *Forbes* and the other from *The Atlantic*. Pointing to the articles, she explained that "the very conservative JPMorgan Chase and even Goldman Sachs now allow casual dress in certain sectors. And casual Fridays are becoming casual Monday through Friday in many companies. It's not that the Silicon Valley boys and younger workers don't have the money for our fine line," she continued. "Some have so much they're just looking for ways to spend it! But, unfortunately, they're not going to buy dress shirts."

The reason for Danica's story now became obvious to all. She ended her narrative with, "Because Blockbuster didn't open their eyes to what was going on around them, the company now lies in the corporate grave next to others that didn't change with the times." The executives looked at each other nervously. Then Cucelli nodded slowly and thoughtfully, as he carefully tucked the articles into his briefcase. He smiled at Danica and said, "You've said some important things worth thinking about, and I look forward to reading these."

Danica's presentation was brilliant! She worded it in a way she didn't need to gainsay anyone. She made her point all through the power of her passion in telling a story. Everyone enjoyed listening to her, but I could see that a couple of the men were not yet convinced. One grumbled, "We understand what you're saying, Danica, but our line is very costly, and casual products couldn't possibly reach our price."

"Oh, forgive me," she laughed. "I almost forgot to mention something else. I'm definitely not about to suggest we go into the T-shirt business . . ." At that, a few of the men gasped. "But here are some other tidbits I found online. (She obviously hadn't forgotten anything, because she'd come prepared with a few printouts of online ads.) She showed one advertising a Fendi T-shirt for $500, a Gucci for $690, and an Armani for $780. All the executives blinked, and to me their eyes looked like clinks of a cash register.

Could Danica have swayed them simply by jumping in talking about today's more casual corporate environment? From my experience hearing hundreds of business presentations, I don't think so. She'd cleverly warmed them up with a personal story dramatized by gestures, laughter, and exuberance. She delivered her research passionately and topped it off with some surprising figures. She held the group spellbound by her storytelling and presentation.

Was Danica really thrilled when Blockbuster opened its doors? Had she really paid exorbitant sums for tapes of her favorite movies? Did she really rent dozens of movies from Blockbuster? I'll never know, and I didn't ask. But I do know that she used a very effective technique to get six stodgy old executives to move in the direction she wanted.

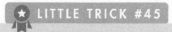

★ LITTLE TRICK #45

Sell with Stories

When trying to bring bosses and colleagues around to your way of thinking, consider more than just the facts. Stories sell. You may not always be able to think of one, but choose an approach that allows you to express emotion. Make your points with excitement and gestures. Whether it's in front of hundreds or just a few, stories engross and passion sells.

42

Grammar Snobs
Can Kill Careers

I t's sad but true: Even if you're the most honorable and trust-worthy employee your company has ever had the good fortune to hire, coworkers and especially management can be blind to your talents if you don't speak in ways they're comfortable with. For many jobs you must be a high school graduate. When you aspire to be a teacher or scientist, you'll need a bona fide college degree. To be an anthropologist or biologist, a PhD is suggested, and if you've set your sights on being a doctor or lawyer, med school or law school is a must.

And although you don't go to school for it, there are certain jobs in our society that call for just a touch of—here comes a taboo word—"class." As sociologist Paul Blumberg wrote in *The Predatory Society*, class structure is "America's forbidden thought," and in the land of the free, it's almost a dirty word. However, since this book is about communicating at work, I'd be remiss if I didn't mention it as it relates to certain occupations. One of the most obvious aspects of, ahem, class is how you speak.

I have a dear friend, Archie, a man of fine character and the highest integrity who, for many years, was a fund-raiser for a school for troubled teens. Archie's a little rough around the edges, but I couldn't care less. I admire his dedication to impoverished high school students, ensuring they have safe housing and nutritious meals. Archie is a truly good human being who deserves great respect and appreciation. Unfortunately, the school where he worked was downsizing and he found himself out of a job.

Wanting to console him, I invited him to lunch the following week. The minute I saw Archie, I was surprised, because instead of being gloomy, he bounded into the restaurant with bright eyes and a big grin, telling me about a "dream job" that had just opened up. "Foxbury is looking for a fund-raiser!" he exclaimed.

"Foxbury?" I asked.

"Oh, you haven't heard of it? Irregardless, it's the classi-est prep school in New York, and I'm a shoo-in. I've been in the school fund-raising biz for over 15 years, and there isn't no better candidate for the job. Anyways, I'm perfect for it because I raised lots of dough for the state school and know the fund-raising biz like the back of my hand."

"That's fantastic, Archie. What would you be doing at Foxbury?"

"Well, I'll be working with a lot of high-class people. I'll have fancy lunches with graduates that have more money than they know what to do with. Well, I can sure help 'em with that!" he chuckled. "They'll give it to Foxbury!" As Archie talked, my heart fell as I thought, "Well, he isn't the most polished spoon in the drawer, but I really hope he gets it."

The following week when he texted me that he'd been passed over, I was brokenhearted, but not surprised. Unfortunately, the grammar he'd obviously picked up from the underprivileged teens would have distanced him from his highly educated, wealthy prospects. One "anyways," "irregardless," or using a double negative like "isn't no better" would have turned them off.

There is a lot of bias in many corporate offices, and some executives wouldn't take anyone who made those mistakes seriously. Discriminating? Yes. Biased? Yes? Prejudiced? Yes. But true.

I'm sure your grammar is far better than Archie's. However, since this book is about talking to people at work, I should caution you that there are grammar snobs out there, mostly in upper management. I've spoken with CEOs who'd flinch if an employee said "further" rather than "farther" when referring to distance, or using "since" and "because" interchangeably. I know one executive who internally screams when he hears sentences ending with a preposition like "Where did she go to?" or "Where's he at?" and then there are the "who" and whom" sticklers. Just as you might recoil at the word "ain't," they wince at word usages like those.

Even mispronouncing certain words can be disqualifying. I often travel to Bermuda to conduct corporate seminars and find intense pronunciation snobbery on the island. Saying "ax" instead of "ask" is a common mistake there. Hundreds of times in my seminars I'd hear, "Leil, can I ax you a question?" Sadly, HR people often bypass extremely qualified Bermudians for top management positions due to a little faulty grammar or pronunciation.

LITTLE TRICK #46

Flawed Grammar Will Getcha Every Time

Watch out! Grammar snobs can catch you anywhere, anytime, whether in writing or speaking, and keep you from reaching the heights you deserve. "What's this got to do with *my* job?" you might well ask. "I'm not working for an upper-crust company. If I spoke differently, it would sound snobby." And yes, it might. However just a heads-up: watch your words at work, because a few incorrect ones can knock you off the promotion track and leave you wondering why.

Nobody's going to say, "I'm not promoting you because of the way you speak." But it happens, a lot. Probably more often than you think.

43

Are You Credible?
(or Just, Like, Credible?)

While talking about credibility, please indulge me while I get this personal gripe off my chest. It may be one of your pet peeves, too, but even if it isn't, give it a quick read, because many people, especially younger workers, don't realize one little four-letter word can smash their credibility—and it's not an expletive.

At a consulting assignment last month, I was walking down the hall behind two employees gabbing away about the day's activities. I overhead one woman say to the other, "Geez, I was, like, really exhausted this afternoon. It was just after my lunch hour, and Lisa, like, comes up to me and asks, 'Are you still on lunch?' I decided, like, to be really nice, and asked her if there was something I could do for her. She was, like, pretty cool about it. But is it, like, any of her business if I'm on lunch hour?"

What level positions do you think these two employees held? Were they respected leaders in the company? Were they top managers? Were they successful salespeople? Or did you figure they were lower on the totem pole?

If you guessed the last category, you're right, and I'm sure you picked up on the dead giveaway. It was the overuse of the word "like." Several upper management executives have told me it hurts their ears every time they hear it, which is pretty often in some companies. To a growing number of clear communicators, you saying "like" is as painful as hearing fingernails on a blackboard. Some managers joke with me that it's a substitute for having a vocabulary. Sure, it's a fun word in certain circles, but not in the upper management crowd you deserve to mingle in. The solution?

★ LITTLE TRICK #47

"Like," Forget It!

Do a mental "search and replace" every time you're tempted to say "like." Then substitute a split second of silence. (Parents and grandparents, if the kids say "like" incessantly, give them a gentle "I'll wash your mouth out with soap the next time I hear it" threat. Get them out of the habit now in case the banal buzzword is still around when they enter the workforce.)

Apologies, I can't resist. Let me share one more phrase that detracts from your sounding like a serious professional.

No Problem!

It seems a verbal virus is spreading across America and expanding at an alarming rate. The cause of the disease is not known, but it is highly infectious among the young and primarily affects those born after 1990. Top professionals over 40 find it especially annoying.

It's called the "no problem syndrome." To most quadragenarians and older, hearing "No problem" in response to their "Thank you" *is* a problem. In fact, just this morning at a coffee shop, I asked the server for some sugar. With a big smile, she replied, "No problem." Her saying "no problem" is tantamount to saying, "I usually do find it is a problem to get sugar for a customer, but in this one particular case it's 'no problem.'"

★ LITTLE TRICK #48

"No Problem" Is a Problem

OK, dear younger readers, thanks for letting me vent. I know you mean well and are sincerely trying to be polite. Take heart from this: before long, all of us born before 1975 will be dead, and you can say "no problem" to each other for the rest of your lives. In the meantime, when we thank you for something, please substitute, "You're welcome." (And if you really want to impress us, say, "It's my pleasure.")

44

How to Lose Credibility Fast

I'm sure you've got a few beefs concerning your job. We all do, present company included. Fear not, I'm not going to bore you with mine, and I highly suggest you keep yours to yourself, too. But if you find yourself with a lot to complain about, if it's any consolation, it may not be your fault. You can blame it on your ancestors! The *Journal of Abnormal Psychology* (sorry about that "abnormal" part) published a study pointing the finger at genetics. If your uncle or great-grandmother was a griper, you're only doing what comes naturally to you. Due to brain structure, some individuals have a tough time putting a positive spin on situations, but even if they come from a clan of complainers, they should bite their tongues at work. No matter how justified they are, kvetching doesn't raise them one iota on the respect meter, and here's the scary part. In a study called "Negative Thinking and

Interpersonal Problem Solving," researchers proved that their subjects' negative mindsets prohibited them from coming up with a fraction of the solutions that positive thinkers did.

Let's imagine it's freezing outside and the heating stops working at your company. The addicted fault finder moans, "We're totally screwed. We'll freeze to death, and knowing this company, it'll take a month to fix it." Instead of adding your voice to the chorus of complainers, wrack your brain for a way to drain some of the pickle juice everyone's drowning in and take action. The CEO of one company I consulted for praised an entry-level worker for doing just that. "Last year, the air conditioning had been out for a week," he told me. "Everybody was suffocating, but a new hire took it on herself to find an AC rental company. She priced one out, and we rented a few. That gal will go far." He saw her as a problem solver, not a whiner, so guess who'd come to mind when it's promotion time?

LITTLE TRICK #49

Search for Solutions *Before* Reporting Problems

Even if you don't find a resolution to a problem at work, searching for one, instead of whining with the rest, increases everyone's respect for you. Problem solvers are promotion material, and if you find a good solution, your boss's boss and even the top dogs will hear about it soon enough—the grapevine does the job for you. Who wouldn't love an employee who tries to make things better?

Next let me share something else that can mar your professional credibility—and this one has nothing to do with your words, your pronunciation, your expressions, or even your body language.

45

The Mind Does Not Belong in a Cage (but Sometimes You're Trapped)

It's considered inhumane to keep gorillas in concrete cages with no greenery, sunshine, or anything else resembling their natural habitat. So why are some employees put in an environment with unpleasant lighting, and often no windows or plants, for eight hours a day, five days a week, and sometimes a lot more? Having worked for a while in a huge space with just partition panels (a cubicle farm), I suspected the office was designed by a sadist whose sole aim was to make the cubicle dwellers irritated with each other. The steady rattle of people tapping away on keyboards, loud phone conversations, banal office chatter, and other distractions are robbing you of peace, not to mention productivity.

Although many companies are moving away from these setups, many employees still work in a tiny office or cubicle. So let's explore how to make yours more pleasant and conducive to getting promoted out of it.

Does a Messy Desk Mean a Messy Mind?

Are you a neatnik at work, or does your desk resemble mine and look like a tornado just passed through? Some people say the latter is a sign of a creative mind. In fact, J. K. Rowling wrote her first Harry Potter books scribbling on napkins in a cluttered coffee shop, and Albert Einstein was an incurable desk slob. In fact, he bragged about it, saying, "If a cluttered desk is the sign of a cluttered mind, what is an empty desk the sign of?" Well, I don't deign to put myself in their esteemed category, but reading that made me feel a bit better about my disorderly desk. Yes, many creative types are office slobs, but that aside, let's talk about what's best for you and your success at work.

Several years ago, Haley, a meeting planner considering me for the keynote address at a large industry convention, asked me to meet her in her midtown office. Walking in, I noticed her desk was completely clear except for her computer, a pencil holder, a stylishly designed inbox-outbox combo, and a few papers neatly piled next to a mouse pad. "Wow, I wish I could keep my desk like that," I remember thinking, "Mine is as cluttered as a crow's nest." We chatted for a while, and Haley told me her time was tight, but she'd be working from home the following week and could I meet her there. "Of course," I said.

When I arrived at her house the next Tuesday, the housekeeper took me up to Haley's home office, and my jaw dropped as I entered. The first thing I saw was a half-open file cabinet with its contents strewn all over the floor and mountains of papers obscuring the surface of her desk. She greeted me warmly and moved a pile of books so I could sit on the couch, which had a discarded Coke can under it. Haley must have noticed my expression. "Oh, don't mind this mess," she chuckled. "It's the only way I can find anything. I'm so much more comfortable here than at the company."

The meeting went well, and I got the gig, but I left scratching my head over the chaotic clutter at home compared with her clean corporate workplace. It piqued my curiosity and inspired me to do further research on the subject. Practically all studies on clutter, including a landmark one published in the prestigious *Journal of Psychological Science* (with a long title, "Physical Order Produces Healthy Choices, Generosity, and Conventionality, Whereas Disorder Produces Creativity"), report that a cluttered cubicle or office makes you less respected by colleagues, customers, and anyone visiting you. True or not, a clean desk broadcasts, "I am organized in my work and in my thinking." If people see your workspace is sloppy, they suspect your work might be, too. Fortunately, I now work at home, usually in the wee hours of the night, and as much as I love my editor, I've never invited her to visit me there.

Your Showroom

Don't go overboard, but by making this an official "technique," I hope to push you in that direction. A showroom is where you show off your product, and your product is *you*. That's the most important thing you're selling. Would you buy a car from a dealership that looked like a traffic jam, or clothing from a shop that looked like a Goodwill drop-off? If people visit you regularly, keep your workspace tidy, because some coworkers will be just looking for excuses to bad-mouth you.

Here's a postscript to the story. Rereading this chapter last week inspired me to put my disastrous desk in order. It was a big job; afterward, I fell into bed exhausted. But lo and behold, when I entered my office the next morning, my eyes lit up with joy. My clean desk saved me the usual half hour of digging through my debris from the previous night, and I was able to dive into work immediately. As much as I hate to admit it, that's a big incentive to keeping an orderly workspace.

Here's something to look forward to, and it's closer than you think. Before long you will be able to design your own augmented reality (AR) workspace and put anything in it anywhere you like. If you're more comfortable with a pile of books, papers, and other paraphernalia scattered everywhere on your desk like I am, you'll be able to create it for yourself. What about the rest of your office? Would you like the lush, calming sounds of water hitting rocks to drown out your noisy colleagues? A view of all of Paris from the top of the Eiffel Tower outside your bay window? A hologram of your boss in shackles right next to your computer? You can make it all in AR for your private viewing pleasure, and no one will see anything but a clear, organized desk in front of you.

These possibilities are in the not-too-distant future, but for now, let's get back to the reality we're stuck in today. And for many employees, the worst part of that reality is working for a boss and with colleagues who drive them berserk. Let's tackle that nightmare next.

PART V

COEXISTENCE (WITH CRUEL BOSSES AND CRAZY COLLEAGUES)

46

Is This the Section You've Been Waiting For?

Is this where you'll discover a magic potion to transform your malicious manager or snarky supervisor into a peaceful pussycat? Or turn an adversarial coworker into an ally? Naturally you'd like to make your boss a benevolent leader who gives you the respect and recognition you deserve. And make all those backstabbing, gossiping, whining deadweights and drama queens into folks who are a joy to work with. How I wish I had a magic wand to do that, but nobody can change a tiger's stripes. What I can do, however, is give you some shields to fend off the attacks and share insights into your plight to ease the pain. The coping techniques we'll talk about will, in time, effect permanent changes for the better.

Let's talk about your boss first. If you turned immediately to this section (and I understand why you might have), I beg you, please go back and read the previous parts first. Why? Because I'll reference them here, and many of the earlier strategies I gave you will work on bosses as well. After all, they're human, too. (I know, sometimes it's hard to believe.) There truly are good leaders out there who provide encouragement and even help boost you up the corporate ladder. Maybe you lucked out and got an excellent one. If so, I'm extremely happy for you. But even if you're one of the fortunate few, don't skip this section. By the law of averages, you'll someday be bridled by a bummer boss, for a short term at least, so be prepared.

If your current boss is driving you berserk, take comfort in knowing you're not alone. A Gallup poll cited 50 percent of 7,200 employees who quit their jobs did so "to get away from their bosses." Here you'll find ways to tame them so you needn't join the legions of others who quit due to contemptible bosses.

It's not within the purview of this book to tackle extreme cases of abuse, sexual or otherwise. You can't rid people of their pernicious behavior with just words, and if you're stuck in one of those serious situations, you must report it. With the hundreds of high-profile people in public life whose careers have plunged due to outrageous personal actions, organizations realize there's a limit. If you report a violation and HR professionals fail to act, they themselves can be personally responsible. Sharing your story with HR is a big gift to your company, and we'll talk about how to do that shortly. But for now, let's get right to the . . .

Bummer Bosses

Yes, armies of them are out there, heading up departments and companies worldwide. But lest this book rival the length of one of the longest novels ever written, *War and Peace* (an apt analogy), I'll limit this section to the most prevalent types. Poor leadership comes in many colors. You'll find bullies, micromanagers, control freaks, credit stealers, incompetents, recluses, hypocrites, bureaucrats, indecisives, hypercritics, and poor listeners. (Did I leave any out?) If your boss fits only into one of these slots (he or she probably won't), you'll find tons of online experts suggesting how to handle those stereotypes. Unfortunately, like no two snowflakes (or flaky people) are alike, no two bosses are either. The bad ones are an amalgam of agonizing qualities. And they wield a great deal of power over your salary, bonus, promotion, and career goals. You can't change the repulsive nature of these characters, but when you employ a blend of the following little tricks, you come away with dignity, self-respect, and the knowledge that you've taken the best path possible. First, however, let me give . . .

A Shout-Out for Your Boss

I'd like to play devil's advocate for a moment. (Or if you prefer, think of it as "boss's advocate.") Have you ever complained to colleagues about your boss? Have you ever done something in what you considered "a better way" even when directed otherwise? Have you ever folded your arms, looked away, or just grunted in response to what your boss said? What about rolling your eyes, being sarcastic, or snapping back? Your boss is only human, but if you've said anything that showed "attitude," or made her suspect you were questioning her authority or ability, that spells trouble. Most bosses have a big ego, often accompanied by underlying hidden insecurity. They bury their vulnerability under protective armor, but when you pierce their ego, whether on purpose or by accident, you detonate their defense mechanism. Then you'd better duck for cover or prepare for a cold war.

Sometimes we forget that bosses themselves are under a lot of pressure. They manage not only you, but probably other people as well. I've had bosses tell me they sometimes feel like they're running a daycare center with all the whining and unprofessional behavior they see. Even if you've done nothing wrong, your boss's exasperation with other employees can rub off. And guess who they take it out on? Right, *you*. So naturally, you take your suppressed anger out on them, but your boss could be the wrong person because . . .

Your Boss Has a Boss, Who Has a Boss, Who Has a Boss (Right on up to the Top)

It's easy to assume the buck stops with your superior, but that's seldom so. She tells you to do something, and you usually do it. You may feel that even asking "Why?" sounds impertinent. Do you remember when you were a kid and your mom told you to do something? You put your hands on your little hips, looked up at her, and asked, "Why?" Sometimes her answer was, "Because I'm your mother. That's why."

Nothing has changed. Your boss may tell you to take an action that makes no sense at all. You may even think it sounds detrimental or risky to your department, the company, your customers, or all three, so you ask why you should do it. She then gives you a corporate-speak response that leaves you blinking. In different words, what she's really saying is, "Because I'm the boss. That's why." Most likely, however, she's just answering to the "powers that be" up the chain because a lot of stuff you don't see goes on at any company. There are things you have no way of knowing, and sometimes your *not* being told is for your own protection and peace of mind.

"But wait a minute," some of you might say. My boss owns the company, so of course she calls the shots. Well, even the top dogs get significant pressure from shareholders, boards of directors, their own HR department, or high-level clients. There is always someone to answer to.

Your Boss Has a Boss

And that boss may be worse than yours! I learned the hard way that business can be a dog-eat-dog world. No doubt there's an even bigger boss gnawing at your boss's heels and keeping him from being the type of leader he wants to be. Practically all bosses have someone they report to watching their every move, and so on up the totem pole. Keep this in mind whenever dealing with your boss, and have a little compassion.

Why Is My Boss Such a _____ (Fill in the Blank)?

Wouldn't it be great if your boss could handle things rationally all the time and not make you want to tear your hair out? But, sadly, there are tons of circumstances in business where it simply isn't possible. Just one tiny example: A team leader named Tanya in one of my classes shared that she was outraged because her boss told her to cancel a purchase order from her favorite vendor. "If I do that," she complained, "not only will it destroy a long-standing relationship, but I've always depended on that supplier to go the extra mile for me in a pinch. And, besides," she sputtered, "production needs the parts to finish their work. My boss is totally irrational and always changing her mind." Tanya was totally confounded, asking, "Why did she tell me to cancel the order when, just three days before, she asked me to place it?" Sadly, I didn't know the answer either. The next day Tanya returned to work.

About 10:30 that morning, I was surprised to see a message from her in my inbox. She'd e-mailed to tell me she had just learned that her firm was on the verge of acquiring another company that produces the same product she'd given the purchase order for. "So of course my boss told me to cancel the order," she wrote.

That made me think of Fats Waller's famous line, "One never knows, do one?" No, Tanya, sometimes we don't know, but our bosses do. Tanya's boss was simply following instructions from her superior, who forbade her to say anything about the acquisition. When your boss gives you an order you don't understand, please realize he or she could be facing a similar situation. Something's happening behind the scenes that you don't, or shouldn't, know anything about (sometimes for your own good).

Your boss's boss is your boss as well. When you get a confusing command, perhaps your boss is just "toeing the corporate line" and protecting his superior out of respect. If it looks like he's cracking the whip senselessly against your back, it might mean you're being protected from far worse abuse.

The following little trick won't stop the person you report to from being a jerk, but it might give you peace of mind so you can handle it better. Realize that somewhere near the top, you'll usually find . . .

Layers of Poop You Don't See

Try to accept what the boss tells you to do even if you don't know why. Take comfort from the situation now, because when you get to be boss, you'll no longer be protected from smelling it. Worse, you'll have to wallow around in it up to your kneecaps or higher. You know what people say, "Poop always rolls downhill." And when the time is right, it will be your turn to shield your employees from that repugnant substance.

Don't worry—for the moment—about your boss telling you to do something that you think is nuts. I'll give you a way around that nightmare in Chapter 49!

Now let's move on to some bosses who strike fear into the hearts of even the most valiant workers.

47

The Hypercritical
Bully Boss

Consider yourself lucky if you merely work for an inde-cisive, absentee, credit-stealing bureaucrat or hypo-crite. Bullies make your life even more miserable, and many employees who report to one practice their resignation speech nightly. But if quitting is not in the cards for you right now, understanding the nature of the bully-beast alleviates some of the pain. These tyrants are a big problem for every-one around them, including themselves.

The Association for Psychological Science has studied these poor souls and found that many bullies have an "appe-tite for cruelty" and actually expend extra effort to make peo-ple around them suffer. In an unusual landmark study called, quite appropriately, "Behavioral Confirmation of Everyday Sadism," researchers directed their subjects to choose between four unpleasant tasks: (1) kill innocent bugs that they'd placed in individual cups, (2) help the experimenter kill the bugs, (3) clean dirty toilets in the lavatory, or (4) endure pain from ice water. To make the first task even more unpleasant, they showed the participants the device they'd use to do the dirty deed, a modified coffee grinder that produced a distinct crunching sound while the bug was being squashed.

If that wasn't enough to dissuade the subjects, they introduced them to the little critters they would decimate. Each tiny cup was labeled with the bug's name: Muffin, Mike, Tootsie, etc. The individuals who voluntarily chose this were directed to drop the bugs one by one into the crunching machine, push the cover down, and grind them up. (Don't worry; unbeknownst to the subjects, the compassionate researchers had installed shields to prevent the bugs from being mutilated. No bugs were harmed in the experiment.)

Of the participants, 12.7 percent chose the ice water and another 33.8 percent chose to clean toilets. But a whopping 26.8 percent chose killing the bugs themselves, and another 26.7 percent chose to help the researchers do the deed.

Does that mean that more than half your superiors have sadistic tendencies or support such brutal behavior? I'm not saying that, but it does make one wonder if some abusive bosses derive pleasure from being cruel. I've witnessed this sadistic propensity firsthand and cringed, hearing bosses lambasting employees in a meeting:

"I have no idea what you're talking about. Nor does anybody else here."

"That's a ridiculous observation."

"Who hired you?"

"Keep your mouth shut, and open it only when you have something more constructive to say."

Remarks like these naturally catch employees completely off guard, so they either gulp and accept it or shout back. If they're too flustered to do either, some frantically wrack their brains for a response, but if they wait a few seconds without saying anything, they've lost the moment. It's a lose-lose situation. Taking it in silence makes you look foolish, but if you snap back, you appear vindictive and petty. If this has already happened to you with a certain boss, it probably won't be the last time, because such insults are seldom one-time occurrences.

Your defense is to be prepared. I suggest you formulate a calm verbal response *now* so you're not left speechless or you don't blurt out something you'll regret. The beauty of the following little trick is that there's nothing your boss can say afterward. It also hints that you grasped your boss's intent, which was to intimidate you. Rehearse this one-size-fits-all response for the next time, so you're not too flustered to think of one on the spot.

The One-Size-Fits-All "Critical Boss" Comeback

Look him or her right in the eyes and say sympathetically, "I understand what you're saying," followed by your boss's name. Using his name will surprise him, and you merely stated the truth. You didn't look confused. You weren't ruffled. You weren't at a loss for words. Your composure wasn't shaken. You merely stated the facts and said you understood.

I've witnessed this technique used effectively by an engineer named Kyle at a manufacturing firm where I consulted. After Kyle made a suggestion in a meeting, his boss, Seth, pointed right at him and said, "That is the stupidest idea I've ever heard!" Unfazed, Kyle looked his boss straight in the eyes, nodded, and calmly said, "I understand what you're saying, Seth." Kyle came off looking strong, composed, confident, and respectful. Seth came off looking cruel. In fact, his boss was so taken aback that he hemmed and hawed before regaining control of the meeting. As I looked around the room, I could tell his colleagues were thinking, "Go, Kyle, go!"

Think of a few responses to cover the most likely situations at your workplace. Do it now while you're feeling no rancor or sheepishness, so you can deliver them in the same calm manner at those difficult times.

48

When Your Boss Goes Ballistic

One of my first consulting assignments was Winners Sports Shoes, where I met a supervisor named Daphne. Whenever I was walking with her, something odd happened. Employees heading our way often ducked into another office or turned to go the other direction. There was a mysterious tension whenever Daphne was around, and I soon found out why.

Once while walking by her door, I heard a big crash coming from her office and an earsplitting scream. Fearing someone had been harmed, I raced in only to see a wide-eyed Daphne behind her desk clutching a hiking boot in her right hand. She hurled it furiously in my direction shouting, "They screwed up again! It was supposed to be a double-gusseted tongue. Those idiots! How are we going to sell this piece of crap?"

I nervously picked up the boot and examined it, trying to figure out what the heck a double-gusseted tongue was. Seeing my confusion, Daphne shouted, "Get out of here, you know-nothing twit!" and hurled the other boot in my direction. I ducked as it whizzed over my head, and I raced breathlessly back to where other employees were working. Seeing me obviously shaken, Daphne's assistant came up to me saying, "Don't worry, Leil. Every day she freaks out about something. Sometimes twice a day." Just ignore it. The president of the company happened to be walking by at that moment and called me aside, saying, "Daphne is excellent at what she does but flies off the handle a lot. I've told her employees to just ignore it because it will pass. That's the best way to handle her."

During my time there, I witnessed several more of Daphne's temper tantrums, and I agree, not responding is the best choice. I've heard bosses go ballistic over employees letting phones ring too long or forgetting to put paper in the copier, and one supervisor who was on a diet screamed at a report for "always bringing in cookies." I've seen coworkers storm out of the building over a colleague talking too loudly, shriek about food left in the microwave, and yell at a coworker for going into their cubicle. Of course, nobody respects a loudmouth, kitchen slob, or cubicle invader, but people also lose a lot of respect for a coworker who throws a fit over it.

When it's your boss who freaks out, it's hard to ignore. It's natural to chew over every word you heard, but try to let it go. Instead, the next time it happens, picture your angry boss (or colleague) in wet diapers, slamming his rattle on his crib. Then act like a patient parent who loves the little tyke anyway and will soon forget his outburst. Smart moms and dads know sometimes it's best just to ignore it. *Bottom line:* People are only as big as what bothers them.

Ignore Big Baby's Fit

Whether it's your boss, colleague, or customer who blows a fuse, pity the blustering babies and realize that they're suffering more than you. Not only that, but these brats will suffer a lot more later because everyone loses respect for them. Stay silent during their hissy fits, and you'll come out on top every time.

Whatever miserable boss or unmanageable colleagues you're dealing with, I highly recommend using the following Little Trick every day. It has gotten countless employees out of sticky situations and in many cases, saved their jobs.

49

Get It in Writing— Your Own!

S omeday after you've reached the top of the totem pole
and are happily retired, you can write your bestseller
called *Horrible Bosses and Coworkers Who Made My Life
Miserable.* At that time, the following little trick will come
in handy. But now, while you're on your way up to the sum-
mit, the following technique is critical. Many employees who
neglected to use it slipped down the pole like it was slathered
with grease.

Did you keep a diary when you were younger? I did,
and reading it years later, I laughed out loud and asked
myself, "Why did I ever even look at that nasty creep I was
dating?" Or "How could I possibly have trusted that two-
faced so-called friend who spread stories about me?" As a
full-fledged adult in the working world, you probably suffer equally painful realizations. Maybe you wholeheart-

edly supported a boss, until you discovered that she was a manipulative liar. Perhaps you loved sharing your ideas with a coworker until he stabbed you in the back and took credit for all of them.

The important thing to realize is that very few things at work come *totally* out of the blue. There are always early warning signs, but we often close our eyes to them. That's why it's important to keep track of what transpires every day as you're going along. Grown-ups don't call it "keeping a diary." They call it "documenting," and it doesn't need to be more than just a few sentences a day.

Every day when five o'clock rolls around, even if you don't think it's anything special, write a few sentences about what happened that day. As I said, every work predicament starts somewhere, and by writing a paragraph a day, you can take a trip back in the time machine to get to the bottom of it. You can analyze how it started, who's guilty, and why it happened. Daily logging gives you invaluable insight and hindsight that you wouldn't otherwise have. Sometimes you might even discover that you're the culprit. But then, at least you won't fly off the handle at innocent people. Just add it to your list of "Lessons I've Learned" to help you the next time. Making a mistake once is understandable. Making the same mistake twice is not.

Your daily documenting can be very short—until you smell trouble, that is. At those times, spend a few more minutes on it, because it is worth its weight in gold. You'd be amazed at the payback you get from just a little effort.

If you're later blamed for the outcome of a situation and didn't document the details of what transpired, you could lose. Your colleagues and even your boss might try to shift the blame to you. If it comes to "he said–she said," the boss would probably win, because top dogs at any company tend to trust those higher on the totem pole. Without dated documentation, you wouldn't have a leg to stand on.

As an example, let's take a common situation. Say your boss directed you to do something that sounds fishy to you. Slapping your forehead, you think, "He's got to be kidding!" "He's nuts!" "No way!" "This is ridiculous!" You contemplate confronting him to ask if he cleared it with his superiors. "No," you think. "That could come off as insubordinate, like telling your boss, 'I don't trust you.'" But you must make sure you're not held accountable. Your contract doesn't say you need to be the fall guy doing what you're told blindly. Your boss didn't hire you because he needed a robot. You were hired because you have the knowledge and skills that make you great at what you do. Sure, follow your boss's directions, but arm yourself with your "Work Diary." As soon as you receive the request . . .

- Document the directions precisely, including what time you were told and how he suggested you go about it.

- Include dates and any important specific words your boss said.

- Read it again, edit out your emotional reactions, and file the priceless document away. It could save your job someday.

Now phase two. If you're still queasy about it, send your boss an e-mail summary of what you were asked to do, but give no hint you're disagreeing. Say it's because you want to understand clearly so you can better perform the task. It could go like this: "Thanks for taking the time to go over the project you assigned me today. To assure I've grasped the nuances, here's a summary of our discussion and the action items. Please make any corrections, or if this is right, just give me the go-ahead. I look forward to getting started."

Now you needn't lose any sleep over it or wonder if you should follow your boss's crazy directions. Just document it for yourself, e-mail your boss for confirmation, and then bite the bullet and do it. It's proof you were performing your job in good faith as instructed. Let's hope you never need it, but, hey, if it later hits the fan, you won't get splattered.

★ LITTLE TRICK #55

Keep a Daily Work Diary

Memories fade and get distorted. Documents don't. Typing a few sentences a day lets you go back and get the story straight for whatever happens at work. When your nose tells you something stinks, document the heck out of it. E-mail a copy to yourself at your home address or file it (password protected) away forever in the cloud. Whether it's a situation with your boss or a sticky wicket with a colleague, it all starts somewhere. Make daily documenting a regular part of your workday.

Now let's talk about another common type of chieftain who drives you crazy by meddling with your every move.

50

Is Your Boss a Control Freak, or a Freak out of Control?

Sometimes it's hard to tell. But pity the micromanagers of the world. Like bullies, they too are deeply troubled and try to hide their embarrassing little secret. What's theirs? Usually a severe case of insecurity, which many conceal successfully. But they're an unhappy lot and continually check on you because they're scared that they're going to fail. Micromanagers inspect your every move with a magnifying glass and take out their trepidations on you. They're in a constant state of panic that you'll forget something or do it the wrong way, and it will reflect on them. The safer you make them feel about themselves and everyone else who reports to them, the better it is for you.

If it's any consolation, micromanagers in large organizations seldom reach the peaks because it's obvious to their superiors that these poor souls lack the essential confidence to make them top talent. Plus, the senior leaders know that bossing you around takes so much of the micromanagers' time, they don't have any hours left to tackle the bigger challenges. After all, if they can't even effectively handle their own department without being on top of everything, how could they run the company? Wise leaders know that the bizarre need of micromanagers to control their employees' every move stifles these managers' productivity and dampens the enthusiasm of anyone who reports to them.

There's a third reason to pity micromanagers. They feel overworked! Don't they realize they have a team who can do the job just as well, probably a lot better than they? No, they don't. But that's their loss.

Imagine your micromanager as the evil plant in the Harry Potter books. This plant, called the Devil's Snare, constricted and strangled everything unlucky enough to be in its reach. If anyone struggled or resisted the Devil's Snare, it exerted an even greater force, binding the victim's arms and legs and eventually squeezing the resister to death. Likewise, the harder you struggle against your micromanager, the more tightly the creepers and tendrils will squeeze you. Thanks to his friend Hermione, Harry discovered that the only way to loosen the Devil's Snare was to be fearless and calm. Like the wise Harry Potter, realize that struggling and resisting is to no avail with this type of boss. You must dig right down to the roots of your micromanager's insecurity and obliterate the fear it feeds on. In short, you must protect your micromanager and make her feel confident that you can handle the situation. Insisting "I can handle it myself" is even worse and will only makes her squeeze tighter. You must have patience and take it in steps, but your well-thought-out plan will be well worth the effort.

First, discover what your micromanager *perceives* is the threat. Not necessarily what it really is, but what she thinks it is. Many people say, "Perception is everything." Once you identify the fear, set her heart at rest that you are taking care of that particular issue. Let her know it's under control and proceeding well. That way you beat her to the punch before she comes sniffing around several times a day. Suggest sending her a very short daily report about what you're working on. Say it's for your own sake because you want to make sure you're on track. Then, in each message, address what your inner psychiatrist has determined is your micromanager's biggest fear first.

For example, let's say you know the most important thing on your plate now is submitting the specs for a new product. But your detective work has uncovered that your boss is really freaked out that you won't have information collected for the annual report. So highlight that first in your daily missive to her. Chances are she'll just skim the rest anyway, but she knows her beloved annual report will be on time, so she can relax.

Repeat this little trick for several other issues that concern her, and in time, she'll begin to trust you. Depending on the dynamics of your office and your relationship with your colleagues, you might even suggest you send a group report because they're probably suffering her stranglehold as much as you and they might be grateful.

Manage Micromanagers with a Daily Report

Failure terrifies micromanagers. Otherwise, they wouldn't be constantly looking over your shoulder. Use your sleuthing skills to uncover their biggest fear. Then ask if you can send a few sentences at the end of each day listing what you're working on. As always, first highlight what you've determined is their number one anxiety.

They'll begin looking forward to your "Daily Report" and won't be as tempted to poke their noses in everybody's business. It will take a little time, but your micromanager will gradually let up.

A brief note on your personal demeanor with micromanagers. No matter what is happening, never act nervous. Even if your heart is leaping into your throat so you can hardly speak, act calm at all times, like you have everything under control. This is the way to get your boss to relax. It will increase his confidence in you.

When the going really starts to get rough, it's time to pass the ball to HR, which we'll talk about in the next chapter. At that time your documenting will be extremely helpful.

51

Does Reporting a Problem to HR Help?

Like practically all deep philosophical questions, the answer is "It depends." Many restaurants have a coat check at the door where you can leave a bag and get a ticket to retrieve it later. Think of the HR department the same way, except the baggage you should leave at that door is your emotions. HR professionals have seen enough tears and fits of anger to last several lifetimes, and displaying yours destroys credibility. When you decide to take your problem to HR, carefully plan what you're going to say, and then rehearse it with your parents, spouse, significant other, or a sane friend. When you've already purged your first outburst of anger, you can deal more smoothly.

Fortunately, most HR professionals are excellent at their jobs. But even some of these folks prefer not to stir the pot unless they absolutely have to. Like the rest of the human race, they have their own fears, foibles, and office allegiances. Unfortunately, I've met more than a few who don't respect confidentiality when it comes to covering their own behinds, so when you do speak with HR, don't leave any wiggle room on privacy. At the beginning of your conversation, clearly state that what you are about to tell the person is just between the two of you and he or she must not reveal the source. Even though confidentiality is the HR credo, don't take any chances.

A student in one of my supervisory classes had a bitter experience concerning privacy. Trevor, a team leader at his company, told the group he went to HR about his boss because she was overly critical of his whole team and destroying everyone's morale. He said he hesitated a long time before reporting it, but finally decided it was the right thing to do. He started the session by requesting, "Please don't say anything to my boss about this, but . . ." Trevor then presented his thoroughly legitimate complaint.

"About a half an hour later," he continued, "my boss storms into my office, slams the door behind her, and shouts, 'I hear you've been speaking with HR about me. How dare you tell them you think I've been destroying morale!' I was dumbfounded. I thought human resources professionals were sworn to secrecy."

Yes, privacy is part of their job description, but don't take any chances! I'm sorry to report that I've heard dozens of stories like this, and if Trevor had employed the following technique, I don't believe that would have happened.

LITTLE TRICK #57

Swear HR to Secrecy Twice

When you share your problem with HR, get *two* promises that the person you're speaking with will keep what you said completely private. Once before you reveal your information and then again at the end of the session to confirm it. Unless your complaint is in one of the serious categories we discussed, privacy is your right. Protect yourself at all costs.

52

When Your Blood
Starts to Boil

OK, you're pissed off and you have every right to be. The jerk demeaned you in an important meeting. A colleague pointed out a mistake you made right in front of your boss. Then there's that backstabber who said he'd support you on an issue but did a complete reversal. You grind your teeth, roll your eyes, and clench your fists.

Whoa, hold on there a minute! Acting irate at work never solves any problems and makes you look bad, really bad. Your fit of fury lingers in people's memories long after they've forgotten what it was about. It doesn't matter that you're 100 percent justified and have every right to be furious, but when colleagues see fire coming out your nostrils, you go down a notch or two in their estimation.

During a meeting I attended at a client's company, the sales manager, Savannah, was fuming because none of her team had met quota. "You need to push, push, push to close those sales," she said. At one point she looked accusatorily at one employee, saying, "Especially you, Avery." He leaned back stiffly, and everyone saw daggers shooting out of his squinted eyes. He started noisily tapping his pen on the table, and when he rubbed the back of his neck, I saw it was sweaty and red. Glaring down the table at Avery, Savannah asked sardonically, "Excuse me, Mr. Anderson, do you have a problem with what I'm saying?" That was the first time I'd heard her call him by his last name.

"Oh no, ma'am. Not at all. Everything is hunky-dory," he seethed. This was the first time he'd called her "ma'am."

"Well, then," she said, addressing the group with a big smile, "I guess we can all get back to making those sales. Remember, push, push, push. Go for it, team!" While everyone was standing up to go, she abruptly snapped, "*Except* for you, Mr. Anderson. I'd like you to stay for a few minutes."

All heads swiveled toward Avery with that "Uh-oh, you're in the doghouse now" expression. I, too, left, knowing he wasn't going to like what was in store for him. Yet Avery hadn't said one word during the meeting. He didn't have to. Hostility and anger oozed out of every pore in his body. If only he'd used the next little trick, Avery could have returned to work with the rest of them and wouldn't be in the kennel now.

The brain-body connection is uncontested. When you are angry, your jaw tenses, your fists clench, and your muscles expand for battle. This surprises your brain, so it asks,

"Whoa, body, what are you doing? You look really angry." To stay connected, your brain follows, and now you're in a fit of *physical* and *mental* anger. But no matter how justified, displaying anger at work makes you look weak.

Since your body is easier to control than your brain, tell your body to reverse its habitual physical instinct and take the lead. Force yourself to inhale deeply, relax, and loosen your shoulders. Your brain notices and says, "Whoa, body, you don't look angry anymore!" In response, your body shrugs and tells your brain. "I'm not. Just look at me. Can't you see I'm not angry?" Good for both of you! Your body faked calm, and thanks to the brain-body connection, your brain tagged along. You're no longer mad, and now you look like you can handle whatever comes your way.

★ LITTLE TRICK #58

When Livid, Let Your Body Lie

It's easier to control your body than your brain. So when you're annoyed with a colleague, customer, report, or boss, first force your body to loosen up. This tricks your mind into making your anger dissipate. Sure, you can slam your fist into the pillow that night to let off steam, but use this technique to keep your anger out of the office. No matter what, you must always look like you're completely in charge.

In Avery's case, it was his boss, but it goes for everybody you deal with on the job: the colleague who keeps borrowing things and doesn't return them, your desk mate who listens to music blasting out of her earbuds, or the customer who places a big order and then changes his mind. Naturally, you must later sit down with these flaky folks and tell them what's on your mind. But tricking your brain into relaxation mode makes you look totally cool, like you're just having a friendly chat with whomever is driving you nuts.

53

When You're Unjustly Accused

Has your boss ever accused you of something for which you are totally innocent? Probably, and when that happens, it really sucks. How did you handle it? Did you tell your boss she was flat-out wrong? Did you stay silent and take one for the team to avoid sounding defensive or argumentative? Or like many, did you try to put part of the blame on someone else?

> "It's not my fault we're over budget. The vendor raised the price."

> "It's not my fault I didn't get the order. The client didn't like the new return policy."

> "It's not my fault the product didn't work. You told me we had to shorten the quality control time."

When asking my students if they've ever been unjustly accused, I hear groans around the room. After I've given them time to get it off their chests, I ask, "How did you handle it?" Many said they'd confronted their bosses immediately, declaring their innocence. Others wrote to their superiors, saying it wasn't their fault. One administrative assistant told me she wrote to the president, saying her boss was "always making false accusations." Ouch.

Spouting "It's not my fault" makes the speaker sound childish and defensive. Most bosses don't really care whose fault it is anyway: they're just frustrated about the situation. Sadly, they often need to vent and lash out at the closest suspect—you.

So when falsely accused, what should you do? If it is truly minor, just let it go. Taking it on the chin is tough, but it shows you have the big picture in mind. Besides, chances are the boss will later discover it wasn't your fault, and then you look like a hero!

But let's suppose the wrongdoing is of some significance and your reputation is on the line. Now you must clear the record and avoid a stain that could hold you back from good performance reviews, salary increases, or future promotions. Here's how.

Say something like, "I can absolutely see how it might appear that way." Or "I understand why you thought that." That's the first step.

Now this next one is important. *Pause* and let that sink in, because your momentary silence says a lot. (The power of the pause again.) Only then do you move on to describe what you believe happened. If your boss deduces that he, she, or another employee was at fault, fine. You haven't named names and don't come off as a tattletale.

★ LITTLE TRICK #59

Rise Above the Fault Line

At all costs, avoid the childish words, "It wasn't my fault." The beauty of saying "I can see how it might look that way" relieves the boss of feeling guilty of making an unjust accusation. In fact, she may feel a bit sheepish about the whole thing. Either way, you sound like a true professional.

I'd like to interject an important point here. Never, ever, go over your boss's head. Top managers tell me they listen, but deep down, they lose respect for employees who break that unspoken corporate rule.

54

When You're Justly Accused (i.e., Guilty)

Oops, now it's a different story. You blew it, there's no wriggling out of it, and you've got to tell the boss what happened. The usual instinct is CYA, but trying to cover yours probably won't be successful and will make you look worse in your boss's eyes. If you played a part in the pickle you're in, own up to it right off the bat. At least your boss can't catch you later covering up or lying about it because you've already confessed. Sure, your honesty might not be appreciated at that moment, but it will be in the long run because it demonstrates character.

If you caused the predicament, you must now take another step, a giant one at that. The minute you recognize the situation is disastrous, don't start dreaming up excuses like the average employee. Think the entire problem through from beginning to end. Do some heavy noodling and come up with various solutions. Maybe they won't be the right ones and your boss won't choose one of yours, but at least she knows you've given it some heavy-duty thought.

Here's an example: Let's say your bad news is that product delivery is going to be two weeks off schedule. Your boss's reaction, shouted or suppressed, is "Why the #@** didn't you anticipate the problem?" Most workers would begin with "But . . . but . . . but . . . ," trying to cover their involvement or share the blame with someone else.

However, you handled it differently. Before setting foot in her office, you prepared a few possible ways to deal with the situation. After laying the bad news at her feet as sympathetically as you could, you said something like, "I underestimated how long the second phase of production was going to take. It's my fault completely. I'm really sorry." (Now she knows you've owned up to it and are not trying to wriggle out of it.) "I'll keep working around the clock to find a way to speed things up. In the meantime, here are some possible solutions I've thought of."

Good, you gave her suggestions and assured her you'll continue working overtime to determine the exact cause of the problem to ensure it never happens again. You've taken 100 percent ownership of the problem and helped defuse the situation. Unlike the average employee, you didn't just dump something in her lap.

Let's compare this with a personal problem that might arise at home. Suppose your little six-year-old comes to you in tears with the shattered pieces of your favorite dish. Which of the following reactions would make you most forgiving? (1) The kid denies everything; (2) he lies, saying his sister did it; (3) he tells you he has no idea what happened; (4) he apologizes profusely and, showing great remorse, holds out a little tube of crazy glue, saying he wants to fix it or pay for a replacement with his allowance?

I'll put my bets on that last little problem solver every time.

★ LITTLE TRICK #60

Suggest Solutions With the Problem

Never report a bad situation without solutions. No matter how deep a ditch you've dug, there's always a resolution. Maybe you don't have the best one, but showing you gave it a lot of thought wins you respect. In fact, come up with several solutions, so if the first one isn't accepted, you have alternatives. That's what consummate communicators who eventually become bosses do. They take responsibility and think of solutions.

55

Get What You Want from Busy Bosses

No matter how many decades of giving speeches and seminars I have under my belt, I still get a case of jitters before starting. Have I forgotten anything? My notes? A glass of water? A timer on the podium? Kleenex? Any props I need for the program?

As I'm darting around like a decapitated chicken, an early arrival to a seminar often comes up to talk. Chatting with attendees is one of my greatest joys of presenting—just *not* in the last few minutes before I start. Can't they see I'm in a frenzy preparing materials? Similarly, supervisors in my classes complain about employees' untimely interruptions.

Sadly, I've found younger workers especially don't pick up on how busy someone is. Why does it seem to be an age-related syndrome? New studies tell us that communicating primarily digitally interferes with the ability to read human emotions, and unfortunately, lacking this skill can hit you right where it hurts, in your paycheck. In a study called "It Pays to Have an Eye for Emotions: Emotion Recognition Ability Indirectly Predicts Annual Income," researchers found a strong link between annual income and the ability to pick up on people's moods. That means people who fully have mastered the next technique are likely to earn more money!

LITTLE TRICK #61

Take a Mental Snapshot

Before asking for a coworker's attention, stop and take a psychic photograph of his face and body. Does he look busy or laid-back? Frantic or fed up? Does she seem to have a "Do Not Disturb" sign hanging around her neck or a welcome mat at her feet? Then approach—or don't.

If you haven't yet suggested Little Trick #33, the "Stoplight Technique," a good catchall statement is, "Excuse me, you're probably busy now and I can wait, but let me know when you have a moment."

56

Wouldn't Work Be Great If It Weren't for the People?

W hen you walk into work each day, do some of your colleagues extend a warm hello or give you a quick smile? No doubt there are a few who just keep on walking, talking, working, or whatever they were doing before you came on the scene. Nevertheless, every single one of them is having an instantaneous uncontrollable reaction to you, positive, negative, or a hundred shades in between.

Likewise, you're subconsciously reacting to each of them. The split second you sense a coworker's presence, especially your boss's, within 10 feet, you have a knee-jerk reaction. Maybe seeing a couple of your colleagues gives you an inner smile and spotting others invokes a yawn. And no matter where you work, there is always at least one who makes you grind your teeth.

In more than two decades of giving corporate seminars, I've met thousands of workers from hundreds of companies. I often ask, "Are there any colleagues you find it difficult to work with?" Responses range from hooting and hollering to a riptide of hands waving in the air. Especially in my public seminars, where participants seldom work for the same company, they feel totally free to vent. And vent they do!

"He cooks stinky fish in the microwave."

"She talks so loud on the phone I can't hear myself think."

"He takes the last cup of coffee and never makes more."

"She comes to work with a cold and leaves her snot-filled Kleenex all over her desk."

When the grumbling goes on too long, as it usually does, I interrupt the session with, "How many of you have talked to the individuals about this?" Now far fewer hands go up, sometimes none. I ask, "Why haven't you talked to them?" The most common answers are . . .

"I don't want to make an enemy."

"It's not my responsibility."

"It wouldn't do any good."

When I explain that there is a way to turn those relationships around, they're probably saying to themselves, "Yeah, sure, Leil, but you don't know this particular jerk at my office. He's an SOB!" Or "She's a witch. Nobody who's sane could get along with her."

You're right, I don't know that person, but I've heard it all. And I do know by developing, nurturing, and augmenting the God-given gifts you already have, plus guidance from these little tricks, you can improve those relationships. I doubt you'll ever be best friends, but at least you can make the workplace more livable for both of you.

If you don't do something, do you think the problem will go away? Will perpetrators suddenly have an epiphany, visit their place of worship, and beg for forgiveness? I don't think so. You must say something to the culprits.

Not wanting to cause bad feelings, many of my students told me they reported it to their supervisor instead. But don't do that *before* you've talked to the individual for two reasons. One, it makes you look weak, like you can't handle the situation yourself. And two, managers usually don't have the time or inclination to deal with matters they feel you should handle. They simply don't want to get involved. A number of them told me that "tattletales" go down a step or two in their estimation because they seem petty. So I strongly suggest . . .

Talk to the Abuser Before the Boss

If you go to your boss about a tormentor who's driving you bonkers, I practically guarantee the first question you'll be asked is, "Have you talked to him about it?" If your answer is no, you look powerless and not competent enough to handle the problem. Neither of those qualities puts you in the running for a promotion. Talk to the transgressor first.

So What Should I Say to the Jerk?

Obviously, don't approach the culprit when he's in the act of committing the sin and your blood has reached the boiling point. Also, avoid talking to him when you see he's busy working. Choose a time and place where you and the offender are both relaxed, perhaps when the two of you are alone in the break room or lunchroom. Approach casually and, if possible, take a seat, because you don't want to be standing over him.

Now here's the tactic. First, ask if he's busy and if you can talk to him for a moment. Be sure to phrase it so it doesn't sound threatening. If he says no, just say, "OK, we'll make it another time," and leave graciously. If you do get the go-ahead, use his name and say, "This is awkward. However, there's something I'd like to ask you. I hesitate to mention it,

but when I'm around, could you find a way not to _____?"
(Fill in the blank with the irksome thing he does.) Say it
pleasantly and nonaccusatorily, and tell him why it disturbs
you. Depending on the situation, you may have to adapt this
a bit, but keep the words "hesitate" and "it's awkward."

The Script for Human Headaches

The key to handling colleagues who drive you cuckoo
is to let them know you "hesitate" to bring it up and
you "feel awkward" about doing so. Your words can be
straight, but keep your body language warm. After saying what and why it bothers you, insert something like,
"Perhaps I'm the only one it disturbs, and I apologize for
that." However, use that one with caution because the
culprit may say, "It doesn't bother anybody else."

If this annoying soul blatantly refuses to change, end
with a friendly "I understand. I'm sure I have habits that irri-
tate a few of the people I work with, too. Thanks for listening." *Now* you can tell your supervisor, saying of course that
you've already talked to the individual.

57

Gagging Coworkers You Can't Stand

She's heading your way with that all-too-familiar "I can't wait to tell you" expression on her face. You brace yourself for another painful concert of moans and groans. You try to be compassionate because you know that, deep down, complainers crave acceptance and are looking for ways to bond with you. These poor folks think that they have no control over what happens to them and that the problem is always someone else's fault. They're just defenseless victims of the boss, the company, the department, or the ever-popular unspecified "they."

In addition, doomsayers feel thoroughly justified in bringing the catastrophe to your attention. I mean somebody's got to, right? Otherwise the disaster would get worse, and worse, and worse. (Of course, they'd love that! More to gripe about.) I'm sure the last time the bellyacher bent your ear, you wanted to scream, "Welcome to the real world, baby. Learn to suck it up like the rest of us!" But you wisely decided that wasn't the best choice for workplace harmony, and you resigned yourself to another time-sucking, energy-draining whining session. Who's going to be dissed this time? The boss? The accounting department? HR? Production? Sales? Or management in general? Anyone except themselves.

Previously when the grumbler trapped you, you probably asked, "Well, what are you going to do about it?" But he never has an answer because he revels in feeling helpless. And indeed he is. So once again, the pessimist plops down at your desk without an invitation. (Disparagers tend to sit down because they plan to be there for a while.)

The solution? Some experts suggest you hear snivelers out and permit them to let off steam. As benevolent as that suggestion sounds, it's professionally dangerous because anyone seeing you babbling with bellyachers might think you agree, and that makes you look bad. If you're both walking and it looks like you're going to be trapped, duck into the restroom. If one is approaching your desk, grab the phone and make a call, or at least pretend you're talking to someone.

If that isn't possible, try this technique instead. Stay completely composed and repeat each of his gripes back to him almost verbatim. Preface it with statements like, "If I understand correctly, you're saying . . ." (Then repeat the complaint.) Or "I see, you feel that . . ." (Then rephrase the grievance using many of the same words.) Just make sure you don't do it with super friendly body language that anyone could misinterpret as your siding with him. For instance, if he's telling you, "The production department never gets the product out on time," you simply state, "Oh, you're telling me the production department doesn't get the product out on time."

He continues, "It's not my fault. I always get the orders in long before the deadline."

You paraphrase: "I see. You always get the orders in long before they need to be."

He adds, "I don't know what the heck they're doing with them. They're probably just gathering dust on their desks!"

"Hmm," you say, "they may be gathering dust on their desks." Just repeating the griper's words won't give him the satisfaction he's looking for, so he'll soon give up and seek more responsive ears. The beauty of it is that you didn't rudely cut him off. After all, you were listening to him.

★ LITTLE TRICK #64

The Verbatim Shutter-Upper

If avoiding conversation with a complainer is impossible, just repeat what he says as though clarifying that you got it right. This will soon start to annoy the kvetch, and although he can't accuse you of being rude or ignoring him, it interrupts his rhythm, which takes all the fun out of it. He won't stay long.

Another Sneaky Silencer

Here's another little trick for dealing with a griper. After his first few sentences, smile supportively and say, "Yes, I understand how bothersome that would be. Let's get this on paper." Then grab a pen or start a new document on your computer. (At this point, you'll probably see a little "oops" expression on his face.) Write what he's just said, then look back up as though you're waiting for more. After another sentence or two, interrupt him and say, "Hang on for a second. I want to get this right," and then start writing again.

Now he gets really nervous and wonders why you're taking notes. Are you planning to tell the person he's talking about what he said? Or the boss? Or everybody in the office? If he asks why you're taking notes, say, "I just want to make sure I understand the situation clearly." He'll quickly wind down.

★ LITTLE TRICK #65

Write Their Gripes

When you first start this technique, the bellyacher will think you're being supportive. But after a few moments, his paranoia will set in and he'll wonder what you're going to do with your notes. This will makes him nervous, and he'll soon quit.

Put Them to Sleep

If, for some reason, you're hesitant to use the "Verbatim Shutter-Upper" or the "Write Their Gripes" technique, here's a third, which I call "Bore the Bellyacher." As the complainer drones on, respond with nothing more than a series of brief responses like, "Yes," "I see," "Hmm," "OK," but do not say anything else:

> Do *not* agree with him.
>
> Do *not* tell her she's wrong
>
> Do *not* offer your opinion.
>
> Do *not* suggest solutions.

Even if your ideas are good, the sniveler will probably protest: "That's impossible," "It's not realistic," "You don't understand." Instead, as a last resort, give this little trick a shot.

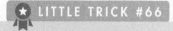

★ LITTLE TRICK #66

Bore the Bellyacher

No matter how many suggestions you offer, dedicated disparagers will relish telling you why it won't work. When you respond with nothing more than a few monosyllabic words, troublesome types get bored listening to themselves and soon walk away on their own.

These three little tricks will at least take you off the list of folks they'll complain to. As they leave your desk, you can take a deep breath and get back to work.

58

Gossiper's Friend Today Is Gossiper's Victim Tomorrow

Is your company . . . considering pay cuts? Reducing benefits? Being sold?

Is your boss . . . having an affair? Talking about layoffs? Getting divorced?

Is a colleague . . . looking for another job? Hiding a prison record? Getting promoted?

If you work for a large organization, you've heard speculations like these dozens of times. And no matter what size your company, you've run into gossipmongers with wagging tongues, loose lips, and helpless targets. These poor souls can't resist dishing the dirt on a colleague's illicit affair or the company's financial woes. They have such a need to spread it around, they wouldn't close their mouths in a sandstorm. Pity the poor blabbermouths, because in many studies like "Why People Gossip: An Empirical Analysis of Social Motives, Antecedents, and Consequences" find that gossipers crave attention and need to make themselves feel superior to other people.

Unfortunately, companies now don't handle rumormongers as effectively as the seventeenth-century Brits did. Once someone was accused of gossip, the British strapped a muzzle— which looked like a horse's bridle, but far more painful—over the storyteller's head. It had jagged edges that kept the gossiper's tongue fixed to the bottom of her mouth. Your company probably doesn't keep a stock of those in the storeroom. However, the following technique is a deterrent for someone who gossips, which is equally as painful for her emotionally. It won't rid her of her habit, but it immunizes you against the verbal vomit. The beauty of it is that it doesn't even alienate the blabber.

Suppose a coworker tells you in a hushed voice, "Don has a drinking problem"; "Heather is leaving her husband"; "Frank said he hoped the manager would get fired"; "Paige gained at least 10 pounds"; "Jackson said that he's looking for another job"; "Karin and Kevin had sex after the last Christmas party." Ad nauseam. Some of my students have found this ruse helpful in such cases: Tell the storyteller that it's interesting, and you'll go ask the person being talked about.

Let's Go Ask 'Em

The next time colleagues start to share a tidbit with you, don't bite and act like you want to hear more. Simply smile and say something like, "Oh really? Let's go ask him about it." The stunned gossiper will start stuttering, "B-B-But . . . " Then you smile and change the subject. The gossiper will get the point.

Get Gossip Guts

It takes spunk not to bite when a juicy tidbit is being dangled in front of your teeth, especially if it's about someone you don't like. If you have the discipline to excuse yourself when you sense trash talk coming, everyone will respect you. Just cheerfully say you've got a lot of work to do and walk away.

Another important reason not to socialize with gossipers? Guess who may be their next victim? The less these story spreaders know about you, the better.

59

How to Skillfully Squash Interrupters

Everyone hates getting interrupted. I do, even when I'm saying something pointless, which is pretty often. One particular colleague who constantly interrupted me comes to mind. I don't think his goal was to torture me. (If it was, he'd let me finish making a fool of myself instead of cutting me off.) After suffering his affront several times, I started watching how other interruptees handled the situation. Some glowered at the perpetrator with a venomous "Ex*cuse* me. I was talking." One looked daggers at the interrupter, pointed to her own mouth, and said, "Hey, lips moving, still talking." I've heard other caustic comments like . . .

"Sorry for talking while you were interrupting."

"Did I take a breath and give you the impression that I'd finished?"

"Now, now, you have to wait for your turn like everybody else."

"If you don't mind, I haven't finished my point."

These rejoinders were meant to squelch the interrupter, but it only triggered uncomfortable silences.

So how should you respond when a colleague cuts you off mid-sentence in a meeting or one-on-one conversation? Here's what I suggest.

★ LITTLE TRICK #68

Kill the Interrupter with Kindness

To make you look like a saint (and the interrupter like a jerk), act like the interruption is not only OK, but that you welcome it. The split second he cuts you off, stop speaking mid-sentence and give the perpetrator an accepting expression. Then look down at your notes or at your laptop. When he's finished, look back up at him and say, "Oh, I'm sorry. I was distracted for a minute." (Of course, you were distracted. He interrupted you!) Then continue with, "Please, I'm anxious to hear what you have to say. What was it again?"

Now the interrupter must repeat what he's said, which makes his intrusion even more obvious. This works especially well in a meeting when he must repeat himself in front of everybody. Then here's the follow-up: Smile as though nothing had happened, and without rancor, state, "As I was saying . . ." Then finish your point. He'll feel like a heel.

60

How to Disagree
Without Declaring War

I'm sure it's happened to you in a meeting or a discussion at work. As soon as you finish making your point, some obnoxious colleague jumps in with "I disagree" or "You're wrong." That's like a slap in the face for no reason. Naturally, you wouldn't say that to your boss, but I can't tell you how many times I've heard employees spit these words out at each other in meetings. Some even respond starting with the word "No," which brings back images of mom slapping your hand when you reached for the cookie jar.

Now let's reverse the roles. Suppose you're in a meeting and a colleague says something that you know is the sticky brown substance that bulls excrete. How do you politely tell Bigmouth you totally disagree with him? And should you?

Of course you should, and if it's an important issue, you must. But do it in a way that retains the coworker's goodwill and keeps everyone's respect. Simply preface your opinion with a few agreeable words—and a long pause—*before* articulating your conflicting views. Here are some examples:

> "You make an interesting point." *Long pause.* Then continue with your view.

> "That's very insightful." *Long pause.* Then continue with your opinion.

> "I understand completely how you could see it that way." *Long pause.* Then continue with your sentiment.

It's even better if you can start your next sentence with "Yes."

> "*Yes*, that's an intriguing way to look at it." *Long pause.* Then continue with your conviction.

> "*Yes*, I can see you've given this a lot of thought." *Long pause.* Then continue with the way you look at the situation.

In all your communicating at work, never forget the power of the pause. Comedians rehearse their timing endlessly because a brief moment of silence gives their audience time to reflect on what's been said, before hearing the punchline. Likewise, give your colleagues an extra second to enjoy your complimentary response before hitting them with the less pleasant part they need to hear.

LITTLE TRICK #69

Commend Before Countering

When you disagree with a colleague, first compliment him with an acknowledgment that his point is "interesting," "insightful," "thoughtful," or any other praiseworthy adjective. Then pause long enough for him to relish the tribute, and only then express your contrary view. He may not even realize that you've just gainsaid him!

61

Before Telling a
Coworker Anything

Do you remember studying ancient Egypt in school? When a humble message runner delivered good news to the pharaoh, he was wined, dined, and treated like a prince. But if the poor messenger had the misfortune to bear bad tidings, the news was even worse for him. Off with his head! The following technique may be obvious to you, and if it is, congratulations. However, I've seen many employees disregard it, much to their detriment, so I want to share it with you.

You never know how somebody's going to react to what you say, so before saying anything, think about how the listener might feel. For example, suppose the president of the company comes to you directly with a matter that usually goes through your boss. You're pretty proud of this, and with a big smile, you tell your boss about it.

Suddenly he turns gruff. "Get out of my office," he commands. Wait a minute, this was a feather in your cap, and he should be pleased. How unfair! You didn't do anything wrong—or did you?

The problem could be the *way* you delivered the news. You've heard the saying "It's lonely at the top." That doesn't just mean leaders regret having less time to spend with friends or family. They are sometimes frustrated that people at work don't understand the intricacies of what's going on, so they have no one to confide in. If you say something to your boss or coworkers without thinking about how they might take it, they can get irritated at you for not understanding.

So how should you have given your boss the news that the company owner came to you and not him? Certainly not the way three people gave me news in just one day last month. Arriving early in Seattle after a red-eye flight, I went to my hotel, where the receptionist chirped, "Oh, your room's not ready yet." (The heck with her smile! How about a little shared disappointment and sympathy?)

Hungry and tired, I dragged myself over to a 7-Eleven to get some cash from the ATM machine. After five minutes of fighting to make it cough up the money, the store owner waltzed over and merrily said, "Oh, that old machine. It's been out all week."

"Why didn't you tell me earlier?" I wanted to shout. (Couldn't he have shared my frustration?)

That evening, I went to my favorite Seattle restaurant, ravenous for its scrumptious signature dessert. I told the server how much I loved it. But with a shrug and a big smile, he chuckled, "Sorry, I just served the last piece." (I fantasized hurling my fork at him for at least not pretending to share my disappointment.)

Why did I react so badly to these situations? Was it the problems? Of course not. Hotel rooms often aren't ready for early check-in, ATM machines go on the blink, and restaurants run out of popular desserts. What infuriated me was the way these people told me. Didn't they know I'd be upset, and couldn't they at least pretend to share my sentiment?

Back to your boss. He could take the company president coming directly to you as a slight to him, so acting proud and happy about it (which you deserve to be) would not be appropriate. Before imparting *any* news to anyone at work, first ask yourself how the listener might react.

★ LITTLE TRICK #70

Tell It Like They'll Take It

You've always heard, "Tell it like it is." Of course that's good advice when it comes to the truth. But here's an emotional lens you should superimpose before making a point. Always ask yourself, "How are they going to receive this news? Will it affect them personally? What complications, confusions, or implications could come to their minds?" Everything that happens at work affects everyone differently, so hear your words through *their* ears and deliver your message accordingly.

62

Don't Bite the Hand
That Signs Your Paycheck

Now let's deal with the number one national workplace pastime. It's fun. It releases tension. It creates camaraderie. Unfortunately, it's also the reason a lot of folks don't get as far as their abilities entitle them to be. So what is this transgression, this violation, this really-screw-up-your-chances-on-the-job wrongdoing? Quite simply, it's griping about your boss. "But everybody does it," you might say. Yes, but chances are those "everybodies" aren't close to the top of the totem pole. When you vent, even if your colleagues agree with you, their estimation of you goes down.

Whenever the "Dealing with Your Boss" segment comes up in my seminars, I see students clench their fists, rub their necks, and cross their arms across their chests. It doesn't take a psychologist to know that these poor folks are in pain. I see sweat on their palms as they wave their hands, dying to tell everyone about their abominable bosses—especially in my public seminars. Their usual grumbling goes something like this: One employee says, "I sent mine three e-mails yesterday. Nothing! She *never* responds." Another moans, "I don't think my boss even reads them." "You guys are lucky," whines a third. "My boss hangs over my shoulder every minute of the day. Talk about a micromanager!" And in every class, I hear things like, "It takes forever for my boss to sign off on projects," "Mine is a spineless wimp because he won't stand up for our department even when he knows it's not our fault," and "I have proof I'm underpaid, but my boss closes his ears, saying it's total B.S."

My training sessions sometimes turn into a contest of who has the worst boss. But there are no winners here. Only losers—the ones who complained to their colleagues about their bosses and got caught. An accounting clerk in one of my classes told the group, "My friend Michelle and I went to the movies one Saturday night a couple of months ago. There was a long line for tickets, so we started just shooting the breeze, talking about our jobs. I was telling her I hated my boss because she's such a bitch. She never stops nitpicking and criticizing me.

"Suddenly, I heard a big laugh behind me. I whirled around and, oh my God, it was the president of the company with his wife!

"'So you think she's the "b" word, do you?' he chuckled. I turned beet red and apologized. But it was OK because he just laughed, and then we made some friendly small talk.

"But first thing on Monday, my boss called me into her office. She was totally irritated and chewed me out for referring to her as a 'bitch.' She said how humiliating it was to hear this from the president and accused me of being two-faced and unprofessional. After that, she started treating me worse and worse. I knew that no matter how hard I worked, she'd never forgive me. So I started looking for another job."

That encouraged other students to spill their sad tales of the consequences when they'd griped about their bosses. A few were transferred to departments they hated. Some were labeled "troublemakers" and never earned back the trust of their bosses. Many were berated and felt sure it ruined their chances for future promotion. Some lost a lot more, their jobs and a good recommendation. So what's the solution? This one is super simple.

★ LITTLE TRICK #71

Never Bitch About Your Boss—Ever

I know, that's like telling you not to breathe, right? But beefing about the boss is a big no-no. Instead, go home, punch the pillow, kick your cat (no, please don't do that!), breathe deeply, and take a long walk. But *never* complain about your boss to a colleague, or even to anyone who knows someone at your company. In fact, I suggest not even griping to any of your personal friends about your boss because it demeans you and makes you sound like you're not in control of your own professional life.

Need I even mention the dangers of griping about your boss or company on social media? Read some of the online tales told by boss complainers. Most of them are now ex-employees of the company where they worked.

As the workplace evolves, some relief is in sight concerning bosses. Although there will always be companies and family businesses where everyone knows "who calls the shots," the corporate world is moving toward a more collaborative atmosphere. The workplace, which is changing at the speed of light, is being influenced by a more socially conscious and socially responsible generation that understands that big data and the Internet of Things connect everybody and everything. Most of the transformations are spectacular, while some are scary. Before we close, let's take a quick peek into what's right around the corner for you at work.

PART VI

CONCLUSION

63

The Office of Tomorrow

Do you remember the story of my dad's office, where I spent my snow days as a kid? The one where secretaries "took letters" for their mostly male bosses and marveled at the new-fangled fax machine? If you were teleported back for a visit, you'd still recognize it as an "office," but if you journeyed in the other direction, you might not.

Let's say you work in the "office of tomorrow." When you arrive, if you're not working from home that day, which you often do, a camera verifies your facial features, the doors open, the AI (artificial intelligence) receptionist wishes you a good morning by name, and your presence is detectable on everyone's device. You walk to your workstation in a spacious room where others, including your boss, are busy on their laptops or other devices. It's a pleasant, more collaborative atmosphere and perhaps includes a coffee bar with stools and a few snacks.

If you jump ahead a few more years, you'll be adjusting your augmented reality (AR) glasses to bring up a monitor showing the new messages that your AI personal assistant has determined merit the best use of your time that morning. If you like, you can also add an AR-framed photo of your family or even a fish tank with a great white shark swimming in it.

You go through your messages quickly because your AI assistant has rewritten the subject lines, giving you the meat of each message before you open it. Additionally, all the information you need to reply to the message is already pulled up.

If you're "old school," you'll want to thank your assistant but then remember it's not necessary because he's virtual. (Or "she." You can give your AI assistant any gender you like.)

Now you're preparing for a video meeting with your manager to review a project proposal. Your AI assistant has chosen a time convenient for both of you depending on your time zones and personal preferences. All pertinent e-mails, documents, chats, and texts are already prepared for you. Your assistant also made graphs look better, corrected formatting, checked the weather at both venues, and suggested what you should say to that particular manager on that specific day to be most effective.

If you get a bit drowsy after lunch, no problem. In fact, naps are encouraged for maximum efficiency. So you book a sleeping pod with twinkling stars and gentle music to awaken you after 20 minutes. Now that you're raring to go again, your AI assistant tells you how to best spend your afternoon.

It all looks good, but in the history of the world, there has never been progress without problems. Many workers will get stressed out, knowing their managers are using big data as a performance metric, and you'll be concerned about accidents on the way to work in driverless cars. Instead of old-fashioned carpal tunnel syndrome from typing, you'll suffer "simulator sickness" in virtual reality. That's the conflict between what your brain and body think they're doing in virtual reality—sort of like the brain-body connection in Chapter 52. Your mind says, "We're moving," and your body says, "No, we're not." The discombobulation results in nausea. But forget the minutia for now; you'll see all this soon enough.

It's nothing to worry about, because overall, in the office of tomorrow, you will be more productive thanks to technology, and you will enjoy an open environment that encourages collaboration with your coworkers. And this book will still be relevant, because despite whatever difficulties or opportunities lie ahead, one thing will never change. Except for robots who help you with repetitive boring tasks, everyone you work with is a thinking, feeling human being.

Now you have the tools to help you reach the top at work. When you have shown that you are a confident individual (Part I) who cares about everyone you work with (Part II) and whose communication is crystal clear (Part III) and totally credible (Part IV), and when you have proved that you handle bosses and coworkers with excellence online and off (Part V), nothing should hold you back—as long as you understand the astonishing animals you work with called "human beings."

64

Understanding the Human Animal

Have you heard of horse whisperers? They are a special type of trainers who have rare insight into the needs and behavior of horses. Unlike the old-fashioned horse trainers, horse whisperers guide the animal with patience and have a profound grasp of equine psychology. With this in-depth knowledge, they gently elicit the horse's cooperation and respect using methods the animal innately understands. In a way, a horse whisperer is a mind reader who knows how a horse he works with feels. Are its ears pulled backward? Nostrils flared? Tail swishing? Hind leg lifted? The horse whisperer knows those signals mean watch out! (Horseback riders with shattered kneecaps obviously missed them.)

The animals at your company are human beings, but the skill set you need is the same. You must watch them carefully, learn to discern the signals each gives off, and try to prevent problems before they start. For many years, I took riding lessons at a stable where a horse whisperer works. Once when Taylor and I were talking, he asked about my job. I told him I did coaching and gave seminars to help people communicate more effectively to express their ideas. I remember joking with him that he was lucky that horses couldn't lie and fake their feelings the way people do.

Taylor thought about that for a while, and then, while saddling a horse for me, he said, "But people can fake their expressions only to a point. If I want to know how someone really feels, I watch them when they're not talking to me."

I felt that Taylor was on to something, so I asked him to continue. "What do you mean?"

"Well," he said, "when people think you're not looking, you get the real story. It's sort of like my job. I watch horses, but they don't act differently just because I'm looking at them." He then turned to me with a wink, saying, "If you want to figure someone out, I guess you should become a 'people whisperer.'"

His analogy stunned me with its simplicity and truth. Lips can lie while speaking, but faces and bodies tell the truth when they think no one is looking. Science pays serious attention to those split-second, fleeting expressions that slip across human faces thousands of times each day, called micro-expressions. By connecting them to brain activity with extraordinary precision, neuroscientists have discovered that it is, in a sense, possible to "read" people's minds—especially if you pay close attention to them when they don't think they're being observed.

I once asked Taylor why people call his profession "horse whisperer." Teasing him, I said, "I've never seen you whisper to any of the horses." He explained that the term came about because, to people who had no understanding of how horses communicate, it looked as though certain trainers were able to walk up to a "wild" horse, whisper some secret message, and gain its respect and cooperation as if by magic.

Wouldn't it be great if you could do that with the people you work with—gain everyone's respect and cooperation as if by magic? In a way, you can, by becoming what I call a "people whisperer." First, let me share more of Taylor's wisdom about horses, and you'll see how it operates with the animals you work with. He continued, "There's nothing magic about it. It's just knowing their animal instincts and understanding why horses react the way they do. You watch how they relate to each other in a herd, and you must catch the signals early if you want to ward off problems. Through practice, you learn how to project yourself so the horse respects and cooperates with you.

"The first rule is you cannot force horses to do anything. You must get them to agree to go with the program. If at some point it breaks down, you must figure out what went wrong, why, and how to fix it. Horses will tell you everything you need to know, but you must keep a watchful eye on them.

"You need to be calm and reassuring when dealing with a horse. It never includes shouting or hitting, because if you lose your temper, all you've done is terrify the horse who will react like any afflicted animal and fight back or take flight."

The words in this final little trick are not mine. They are Taylor's words verbatim. All I've done is substitute the word "coworker" whenever he said, "horse." You can substitute the word "boss" if you like, but "coworker" signifies both.

★ LITTLE TRICK #72

Be a People Whisperer

"There's nothing magic about it. It's just knowing their animal instincts and understanding why *coworkers* react the way they do. You watch how they relate to each other in a herd, and you must catch the signals early if you want to ward off problems. Through practice, you learn how to project yourself so the *coworker* respects and cooperates with you.

"The first rule is you cannot force *coworkers* to do anything. You must get them to agree to go with the program. If at some point it breaks down, you must figure out what went wrong, why, and how to fix it. *Coworkers* will tell you everything you need to know, but you must keep a watchful eye on them.

"You need to be calm and reassuring when dealing with a *coworker*. It never includes shouting or hitting, because if you lose your temper, all you've done is terrify the *coworker* who will react like any afflicted animal and fight back or take flight."

The key to succeeding with people is understanding the nature of the animals you work with and how they react to everything you say and do. But just reading these 72 little tricks won't make you a better communicator on the job. *Practicing* them until they become second nature will. Soon you'll never again need to ask yourself, "How shall I handle this situation at work?" because doing it the right way will be automatic. It's for the same reason I wrote in *How to Talk to Anyone*:

Repeating an action makes it a habit.

Your habits create your character.

And your character is your destiny.

May success be your destiny at work.

A PERSONAL NOTE

I deeply hope this book helps you in your journey through the working world. If you have any questions, suggestions, or comments, I'd love to hear from you. Write to me at Leil@CoolCommunicating.com and I'll get back to you as quickly as I can. You can also sign up for my free monthly tip called "Little Tricks for Big Success in Relationships" on my website, www.Lowndes.com. It's a short once-a-month tip for better communicating in business, friendship, and love.

I wish you all good things in both your professional and personal lives.

Bibliography

Books

Arden, John B. *Rewire Your Brain: Think Your Way to a Better Life*. New York: John Wiley & Sons. 2010.

Allessandra, Tony, and Michel J. O'Connor. *The Platinum Rule: Do Unto Others as They'd Like Done Unto Them*. New York: Warner Books, 1996.

Argyle, Michael. *The Psychology of Interpersonal Behavior*. Baltimore: Pelican Publications, 1967.

Benton, Debra A. *The Leadership Mind Switch: Rethinking How We Lead in the New World of Work*. New York: McGraw-Hill, 2017.

Brinkman, Rick, and Dr. Rick Kirschner. *Dealing with People You Can't Stand: How to Bring Out the Best in People at Their Worst*. New York: McGraw-Hill, 2010.

Cabane, Olivia Fox. *The Charisma Myth: How Anyone Can Master the Art and Science of Personal Magnetism*. New York: Penguin Books, 2012.

Crowley, Katherine, and Kathi Elster. *Working With You is Killing Me: Freeing Yourself from Emotional Traps at Work.* New York: Hachette Book Group, 2006.

Daniel, Donald C., and Katherine L. Herbig (eds.). *Strategic Military Deception.* New York: Pergamon Press, 1982.

Dean, Peter J., and Molly D. Shepard. *The Bully-Proof Workplace: Essential Strategies, Tips, and Scripts for Dealing with the Office Sociopath.* New York: McGraw-Hill, 2017.

Donovan, Jeremy. *How to Deliver a TED Talk: Secrets of the World's Most Inspiring Presentations.* New York: McGraw-Hill, 2014.

Dupont, Kay. *Handling Diversity in the Workplace.* New York: American Media Publishing, 1997.

Ekman, Paul. *Telling Lies: Clues to Deceit in the Marketplace, Politics, and Marriage.* New York: W. W. Norton, 1985.

Festinger, Leon. *A Theory of Cognitive Dissonance.* Stanford, CA: Stanford University Press, 1957.

Fine, Debra. *The Fine Art of Small Talk.* New York: Hachette, 2002.

Gabor, Don. *Speaking Your Mind in 101 Difficult Situations.* New York: Conversation Arts Media, 2013.

Gladwell, Malcolm. *Blink: The Power of Thinking Without Thinking.* New York: Little, Brown and Company, 2005.

Goleman, Daniel. *Emotional Intelligence.* New York: Bantam Books, 1995.

Goman, Carol Kinsey. *The Silent Language of Leaders: How Body Language Can Help—or Hurt—How You Lead.* San Francisco: Jossey-Bass, 2011.

Lewis, David. *The Secret Language of Success.* New York: Carroll & Graf Publishers, 1989.

Lieberman, David J. *Instant Analysis.* New York: St. Martin's Press, 1997.

Mehrabian, Albert. *Silent Messages: Implicit Communication of Emotions and Attitudes* (2nd ed.). Belmont, CA: Wadsworth, 1981.

Morris, Desmond. *Manwatching: A Field Guide to Human Behavior.* New York: Harry N. Abrams, 1977.

Nelson, Noelle. *Got A Bad Boss? Work That Boss to Get What You Want at Work.* New York: Mindlab Publishing, 2013.

Pennebaker, James W. *The Secret Life of Pronouns: What Our Words Say About Us.* New York: Bloomsbury Press, 2013.

Putnam, Laura. *Workplace Wellness That Works: 10 Steps to Wellness That Works: 10 Steps to Infuse Well-Being and Vitality into Any Organization.* New York: Wiley, 2015.

Rao, Srikumar S., PhD. *Happiness at Work: Be Resilient, Motivated, and Successful—No Matter What.* New York: McGraw-Hill, 2010.

Tannen, Deborah. *Talking from 9 to 5: Women and Men at Work.* New York: Avon Books, 1994.

Tumlin, Geoffrey. *Stop Talking, Start Communicating.* New York: McGraw-Hill, 2013.

Walters, Lilly, *What to Say When You're Dying on the Platform.* New York: McGraw-Hill, 1995.

Weber, Craig. *Conversational Capacity: The Secret to Building Successful Teams That Perform When the Pressure Is On.* New York: McGraw-Hill, 2013.

White, Paul, PhD. *The Vibrant Workplace: Overcoming the Obstacles to Building a Culture of Appreciation.* Chicago: Northfield Publishing, 2017.

Wood, Patti. *Snap: Making the Most of First Impressions, Body Language & Charisma.* Novato, CA: New World Library, 2012.

Periodicals

Beersma, Bianca, and G. A. Van Kleef. "Why People Gossip: An Empirical Analysis of Social Motives, Antecedents, and Consequences." *Journal of Applied Social Psychology*, November 2012.

Bem, D. J. "Self Perception Theory." *Advances in Experimental Social Psychology*, 1972, Vol. 66.

Bennett, Adrian. "Interruptions and the Interpretation of Conversation." *Discourse Processes*, November 2009.

Bruch, M. A., M. Fallon, and R. G. Heimberg. "Social Phobia and Difficulties in Occupational Adjustment." *Journal of Counseling Psychology*, January 2003.

Buckels, Erin E., et al. "Behavioral Confirmation of Everyday Sadism." *Journal of Psychological Science*, September 2013.

Burgoon, J. K. "Interpersonal Expectations, Expectancy Violations, and Emotional Communication." *Social Psychology Quarterly*, March 1993.

Carmody, Dennis P., and Michael Lewis. "Brain Activation When Hearing One's Own and Others' Names." *Brain Research*, November 2006.

Cook, Mark. "Gaze and Mutual Gaze in Social Encounters." *American Scientist*, 1977, Vol. 65.

Curtis, Rebecca C., and Kim Miller. "Believing Another Likes or Dislikes You: Behaviors Making the Beliefs Come True." *Journal of Personality and Social Psychology*, September 1986.

Day, M. E. "An Eye Movement Phenomenon Relating to Attention, Thought and Anxiety." *Perceptual and Motor Skills*, October 1964.

Dressel, F., and Paul Atchley. "Conversation Limits Attention: The Impact of Conversation Complexity." *Journal of Vision*, September 2005.

Dunn, Elizabeth W. "Misunderstanding the Affective Consequences of Everyday Social Interactions." *Journal of Personality and Social Psychology*, December 2006.

Eckman, P., and W. Freisen. "Detecting Deception from the Body or Face." *Journal of Personality and Social Psychology*, 1974, Vol. 29.

Eckman, P., and W. Freisen. "Nonverbal Leakage and Clues to Deceptions." *Psychiatry, Journal for the Study of Interpersonal Processes*, October 2016.

Griffitt, W., and T. Jackson. "The Influence of Ability and Nonability Information on Personnel Selection Decisions." *Psychological Reports*, December 1970.

Haase, R., and D. Tepper. "Nonverbal Components of Empathetic Communication." *Journal of Counseling Psychology*, November 1972.

Leary, M. R., and R. F. Baumeister. "The Nature and Function of Self-Esteem, Sociometer Theory." *Advances in Experimental Social Psychology*, 2000, Vol. 32.

Lyubomirsky, Sonja, and Nolen-Hoeksema, Susan. "Effects of Self-Focused Rumination on Negative Thinking and Interpersonal Problem Solving." *Journal of Personality and Social Psychology*, August 1995.

Marcus, Bernd, et al. "The Structure of Counterproductive Work Behavior." *Journal of Management*, September 2016.

Maslow, A. H., and N. L. Mintz. "Effects of Aesthetic Surroundings." *Journal of Psychology*, 1956, Vol. 41.

Momm, Tassilo, et al. "It Pays to Have an Eye for Emotions: Emotion Recognition Ability Indirectly Predicts Annual Income." *Journal of Organizational Behavior*, November 2014.

Moser, Jason. "Biological Evidence of Positive and Negative People in the World." *Journal of Abnormal Psychology*, April 2014.

Nair, S., et al. "Do Slumped and Upright Postures Affect Stress Responses?" *Journal of Health Psychology*, 2015, Vol. 34.

Neuberg, S. L., and S. T. Fiske. "Motivational Influences on Impression Formation: Outcome Dependency, Accuracy-Driven Attention, and Individuating

Processes." *Journal of Personality and Social Psychology*, October 1987.

Petty, Richard, and Pablo Briño. "Body Posture Affects Confidence in Your Own Thoughts." *ScienceDaily*, October 2009.

Shotland, R., et al. "Can Men and Women Differentiate Between Friendly and Sexually Interested Behavior?" *Social Psychology Quarterly*, 1988, Vol. 51.

Smith, Heather J., Dane Archer, and Mark Costanzo. "'Just a Hunch': Accuracy and Awareness in Person Perception." *Journal of Nonverbal Behavior*, March 1991.

Stodgill, R. "Personal Factors Associated with Leadership: A Survey of the Literature." *Journal of Psychology*, July 2010.

Vidyarthi, P. R., et al. "Where Do I Stand? Examining the Effects of Leader-Member Exchange Social Comparison on Employee Work Behaviors." *Journal of Applied Psychology*, September 2010.

Vohs, Kathleen D., et al. "Physical Order Produces Healthy Choices, Generosity, and Conventionality, Whereas Disorder Produces Creativity." *Journal of Psychological Science*, 2013, Vol. 44.

Weber, Lauren. "What Do Workers Want from the Boss?" *Wall Street Journal*, April 2, 2015.

Willis, Janine, and Alexander Todorov. "Making Up Your Mind After a 100-Ms Exposure." *Psychological Science*, 2006.

About the Author

Leil Lowndes is an internationally recognized communications expert who specializes in the subconscious interactions that take place in all interpersonal communications. She has spoken at and conducted hundreds of seminars for major corporations, associations, and the public in every major city in the United States, as well as internationally.

A wide variety of publications have praised Leil's work, including the *Wall Street Journal, New York Times, Chicago Tribune, Los Angeles Times, Time, Psychology Today*, and the Huffington Post. She has appeared as a guest expert on countless national television shows and news programs on the four major networks: ABC, CBS, NBC, and Fox.

Leil is the author of 10 top-selling books on communication skills for business and social relationships, including *How to Talk to Talk to Anyone* and *How to Instantly Connect with Anyone*. Her books have been translated into 26 languages.

For more information, please visit www.Lowndes.com.

Also by Leil Lowndes

LEIL LOWNDES

HOW TO TALK TO ANYONE

92 Little Tricks for Big Success in Relationships